Artificial Intelligence and Project Management

Although some people had doubts about the usefulness of such solutions in the past, artificial intelligence (AI) plays a growing role in modern business. It can be expected that the interest in it will also lead to an increase in support for the planning, evaluation, and implementation of projects. In particular, the proper functioning of multifaceted evaluation methods has a crucial impact on the appropriate planning and execution of various projects, as well as the effective achievement of the organization's goals. This book offers a presentation of the complex problems and challenges related to the development of AI in project management, proposes an integrated approach to knowledge-based evaluation, and indicates the possibilities of improving professional practical knowledge in this field.

The unique contribution of this book is to draw attention to the possibilities resulting from conducting transdisciplinary research and drawing on the rich achievements in the field of research development on knowledge-based systems that can be used to holistically support the processes of planning, evaluation, and project management. The concept of the integrated approach to knowledge-based evaluation is presented and developed as a result of drawing inspiration mainly from the systems approach, generative AI, and selected mathematical models.

Presented in a highly accessible manner, the book discusses mathematical tools in a simple way, which enables understanding of the content by readers across broad subject areas who may be not only participants in specialist training and university students but also practitioners, consultants, or evaluators. This book will be a valuable resource for academics and upper-level students, in particular, across project management-related fields, and of great interest to all those looking to understand the challenges and effectiveness of AI in business.

Tadeusz A. Grzeszczyk is Associate Professor in the Faculty of Management at Warsaw University of Technology, Poland. He engages in scientific and didactic activities focused on scientific research methodologies, encompassing qualitative, quantitative, and mixed methods approaches in the realms of management, social and economic sciences, and evaluation research. His scientific interests span methodological assistance for project and program evaluations, AI decision-support methods, and knowledge-based systems. He has written over a hundred papers and contributed to several books. Additionally, he is a reviewer for numerous journals indexed in the Web of Science or Scopus databases, and evaluates a number of national and international project proposals. His involvement extends to being a member of various national and international scientific societies, editorial boards, and advisory committees.

Routledge Focus on Business and Management

The fields of business and management have grown exponentially as areas of research and education. This growth presents challenges for readers trying to keep up with the latest important insights. *Routledge Focus on Business and Management* presents small books on big topics and how they intersect with the world of business research.

Individually, each title in the series provides coverage of a key academic topic, whilst collectively, the series forms a comprehensive collection across the business disciplines.

Happiness and Wellbeing in Singapore
Beyond Economic Prosperity
Siok Kuan Tambyah, Tan Soo Jiuan and Yuen Wei Lun

Healthy Ageing after COVID-19
Research and Policy Perspectives from Asia
Edited by Wang-Kin Chiu and Vincent T.S. Law

Entrepreneurial Attributes
Accessing Your Inner Entrepreneur For Business and Beyond
Andrew Clarke

Leadership and Strategic Management
Decision-Making in Times of Change
Paolo Boccardelli and Federica Brunetta

Artificial Intelligence and Project Management
An Integrated Approach to Knowledge-Based Evaluation
Tadeusz A. Grzeszczyk

For more information about this series, please visit: www.routledge.com/Routledge-Focus-on-Business-and-Management/book-series/FBM

Artificial Intelligence and Project Management

An Integrated Approach to
Knowledge-Based Evaluation

Tadeusz A. Grzeszczyk

Routledge
Taylor & Francis Group

LONDON AND NEW YORK

First published 2024
by Routledge
4 Park Square, Milton Park, Abingdon, Oxon OX14 4RN

and by Routledge
605 Third Avenue, New York, NY 10158

Routledge is an imprint of the Taylor & Francis Group, an informa business

British Library Cataloguing-in-Publication Data
A catalogue record for this book is available from the British Library

ISBN: 978-1-032-37726-1 (hbk)
ISBN: 978-1-032-37730-8 (pbk)
ISBN: 978-1-003-34161-1 (ebk)

DOI: 10.4324/9781003341611

Typeset in Times New Roman
by Apex CoVantage, LLC

Contents

vi   *Contents*

Figures

Tables

1 Introduction

The popularity and importance of various types of projects are constantly growing in the face of the increasing complexity of the functioning of modern organizations. They often take up the challenge of giving up relatively simple, repetitive, and process-based work organization in favor of focusing on unique and complex projects, the implementation of which means making decisions in conditions of uncertainty.

In practice, uncertain decisions related to the planning and implementation of projects are made using multicriteria expert analysis. This means that companies often need to rely on experts' tacit and subjective knowledge. Apart from that, project management and evaluation issues are poorly structured decision-making problems in conditions of high uncertainty. It results from the increasing complexity of many external and internal conditions of the organization's functioning, as well as the significant variability and turbulence of the project environment. The need to analyze, in conditions of considerable uncertainty, complex and complicated phenomena that occur in a dynamically changing environment forces the use of solutions based on nondeterministic models and artificial intelligence (AI) algorithms.

Although some people had considerable doubts about the usefulness of such solutions in the past, AI plays a growing role in modern business. The dynamic development of new technologies and rich applications of AI and knowledge-based systems (KBS) in business and management indicates that they also create a significant potential for changes in supporting the planning, evaluation, and performance of a wide range of temporary, unique, and complex endeavors. It can be expected that the interest in them will also lead to an increase in support for the planning, evaluation, and implementation of projects. In particular, the proper functioning of multifaceted evaluation methods has a crucial impact on the appropriate planning and execution of various projects, as well as the effective achievement of the organization's goals.

Knowledge-based evaluation may be one of the directions for developing comprehensive approaches and methods, the implementation of which may contribute to the improvement of the quality, effectiveness, and objectivity of project planning, evaluation, and execution processes. The value of this book results from

DOI: 10.4324/9781003341611-1

a synthetic presentation of complex problems and challenges related to the development of AI in project management, proposing an integrated approach to knowledge-based evaluation, and indicating the possibilities of improving professional practical knowledge in this field. The book outlines the general background of such issues, the chosen basic concepts, and the general usefulness of selected AI methods in project management. Its content is intended to encourage familiarity with and use of the proposed integrated approach to knowledge-based evaluation.

Various methods supporting project management and evaluation are of interest to business practitioners and consultants. Classic tools and techniques for assessing investment projects based on quantitative financial indicators are well developed. However, there is a growing interest on the part of practitioners in a scientific solution to the problem of multifaceted evaluation of contemporary sustainable projects (organizational, strategic, social, environmental, etc.), which often requires considering hard-to-quantify phenomena and qualitative criteria. These practitioners understand the limitations of long-standing classic tools and methods in supporting decisions for advanced projects. The impact of scientific research in this field can be supplemented thanks to the proposed solutions based on the extensive achievements in improved information and communications technology (ICT) solutions, data science methods, and machine learning (ML).

The content presented in this book is useful outside the university environment due to the practical usefulness of solutions considering quantitative financial criteria and other qualitative and difficult-to-measure economic, social, environmental, and sustainable development aspects. Research on the use of AI in this area is at an early stage of development. This book briefly describes one of the more interesting research trends related to knowledge-based evaluation.

It is essential to understand the need to develop an integrated approach useful in project management, undergoing dynamic development and a well-recognized field in business and management. As part of this intense and varied research, the relatively new applications of AI are particularly interesting. The unique contribution of this book is to draw attention to the possibilities resulting from conducting a transdisciplinary study based on the rich achievements in the field of research development on KBS that can be used to holistically support the processes of planning, evaluation, and project management. In particular, the concept of the integrated approach to knowledge-based evaluation is presented and improved as a result of drawing inspiration, for example, from learning models for project evaluation, the systems approach, generative AI (GAI), Rule-Based Systems (RBS), and Dominance-based Rough Set Approach (DRSA). The latter supports developing a general model for acquiring knowledge through learning and its use in project planning and evaluation. On the other hand, DRSA provides the possibility of formalizing the considerations regarding multicriteria analysis of projects, proposing the implementation of the model, and conducting empirical research. Applying the suggested approach creates good conditions for the performance of multifaceted and knowledge-based evaluation processes.

The book presents many complex topics and issues related to applying selected AI methods in project management and evaluation in a highly accessible manner. Mathematical tools are discussed simply, enabling understanding of the content by average readers, who may be not only participants in specialist training or university students but also economic practitioners, consultants, or evaluators.

The remainder of this introductory first chapter justifies the book's structure. The second chapter introduces the fundamentals of AI and its significant potential to efficiently process vast amounts of data; discover knowledge from data by finding patterns and similarities in empirical, imprecise, and uncertain datasets; and assist in formulating conclusions from information processing. The following approaches, methods, and systems are presented: ML, and neural networks, GAI, rough set theory, and KBS.

The third chapter briefly discusses the selected AI solutions available to data-driven project managers. The competencies of project professionals should evolve due to the departure from an intense process-adherence orientation and focusing on the search for project success thanks to decisions based on knowledge resulting from large and heterogeneous datasets. New technological opportunities, well-known from computer science, can be used in big data analysis and mining, knowledge discovery, and decision support-selected processes in project management. An overview of the better-known and more recent study results concerning leading innovations and GAI is provided. In addition, learning models for project evaluation, applications of RBS, and methodological approaches for multicriteria knowledge-based project analysis are synthetically discussed.

The fourth chapter synthetically presents the fundamental issues of evaluation knowledge management, knowledge discovery through learning, RBS, and more critical problems related to implementing knowledge-based evaluation systems. Then, the essence of the multifaceted AI-driven knowledge-based evaluation and the proposed integrated approach are discussed. In turn, the general model prepared using this approach is presented. Finally, practical remarks on using such models in multifaceted project evaluation processes are shown.

The final chapter proves that the presented solutions based on the proposed integrated approach to knowledge-based evaluation have significant theoretical and practical values, provide substantial added value to the existing research related to the applications of AI in project management, and indicate opportunities for the development of project professionals in this area. The chapter stresses that their application can contribute to obtaining significant benefits related to various levels of project management. It highlights substantial limitations concerning developing AI applications in project management, particularly one of its new sub-fields, that is GAI and large language models (LLM), and practical applications regarding building and updating AI-powered knowledge bases for evaluation systems. The presented considerations constitute a good foundation for future research and the improvement of knowledge in the field of AI in project management.

2 AI in Business

The Essence and Potential of Artificial Intelligence

AI has been the subject of many definitions, and there is no universally accepted one. It is closely related to computer science and cognitive sciences and is a field that concerns building models, computer programs, and systems referred to as intelligent (computational intelligence systems). Intelligent systems are based on various and often very different AI methods, which were developed using various inspirations (functioning of the human brain, mathematical symbolic calculation, phenomena of biological evolution, and others).

AI refers to situations when a machine performs actions that are considered intelligent and is an extensive field of knowledge regarding artificially implemented intelligence (Kim et al., 2023). This intelligence is referred to as artificial as opposed to the natural intelligence associated with the human mind. Intelligent computer systems are developed to build capabilities in the implementation of selected mental functions and obtain human-like effects, especially in the areas of learning, rational thinking, and solving complex problems in conditions of uncertainty.

The concept of AI is related to dynamically expanding fields of scientific research that concern machine implementations of heuristic algorithms inspired – for example, by biology and mathematics. AI-based technologies and techniques enable scientific research leading to the development of new methods that complement other computer applications. The term 'technology' means a scientifically justified method of using technical means. In turn, technique (from the Greek 'techne' – skill, art) can be understood most generally as the ability to perform various types of activities (related to the use of technical means) in order to produce the desired material goods. Techniques provide knowledge about practical methods of conduct, and the main feature that distinguishes AI techniques from others is the ability to learn, generalize knowledge, and adapt to a changing, vaguely defined reality and to solve ambiguously defined problems.

John von Neumann and Alan Turing are considered to be the pioneers of research on AI techniques. The former made a significant contribution to

DOI: 10.4324/9781003341611-2

many fields of science, including mathematics, computer science, chemistry, and physics. He is primarily known as the main creator of game theory, researcher of numerical weather forecasts, mathematical analysis, mathematical logic, and set theory. In addition, he dealt with quantum mechanics and participated in the American military research and construction Manhattan Project. More and more complex and complicated projects require more and more advanced intelligent tools supporting decision-making in their planning and implementation. Von Neumann's research initiated experiments related to the so-called artificial life. In turn, Alan Turing was one of the first to start research related to neural networks and the artificial brain. He is the author of the article entitled 'Computing Machinery and Intelligence' published in 1950 and is often referred to as the father of AI.

AI is a tremendously vast field, and various algorithms have been developed that are aimed at solving a variety of tasks. These algorithms can therefore be classified in various ways – for example, from the point of view of their ability to solve complex problems. Within this classification, it is possible to distinguish two types of intelligent systems. The first one is based on relatively simple mathematical models, which are called artificial narrow intelligence (ANI) or weak AI (WAI). The second type is called artificial general intelligence (AGI) or strong AI (SAI).

ANI is being practically developed and used more and more widely. On the other hand, other types of AI (e.g., AGI), might be introduced in the future and are currently only the subject of theoretical considerations. AGI is intended to achieve the ability to independently learn solutions to new tasks in a diverse and turbulent environment. Independence means the lack of people's involvement in building models and controlling learning processes. Some scientists suggest that there is an urgent need to address the risks associated with the development of dangerous AGI that could even threaten the fate of humanity. Therefore, attention is drawn to the need to consider undertaking credible and rigorous research on safe AGI design, implementation, monitoring, and management (McLean et al., 2023).

Within what is considered ANI, two types of AI can be distinguished taking into account the functions performed – that is, reactive machine AI (RMAI), for solving simple, specific, and narrowly specialized tasks, and the more advanced limited memory AI (LMAI). The first-mentioned type of AI enables the processing of large datasets and is based on relatively simple mathematical and statistical tools. Using RMAI one can obtain solutions that, with some approximation, can be considered intelligent. RMAI systems have been known for a long time and are used, for example, in email spam filters and streaming services recommendation systems. The most famous are chess-playing expert systems, specifically the Deep Blue supercomputer developed by IBM over 30 years ago, which achieved significant success through statistical analyses of potential moves in a chess game.

As mentioned above, ANI can also include the more advanced LMAI. Limited memory solutions enable the storage of data describing past events, which are used to solve current problems and new tasks. LMAI systems are also utilized in analyses carried out with real-time data. Such systems are currently implemented, for example, to formulate recommendations in AI chatbots and support autonomous car control systems.

ANI is nowadays widely developed in specific narrow areas and usually supports one class of relatively simple tasks, for example, forecasting, image recognition, voice assistance, or information search support. Conducting computational experiments (considered to go well beyond WAI limitations) regarding, for example, autonomous systems operating in unpredictable, dynamically changing environments is considered a significant success (Sifakis & Harel, 2023).

Unlike ANI, AGI researchers have much greater ambitions and attempt to model and implement artificial beings (devices, robots, etc.) that think and behave like people. Such research aims not only to imitate human intellect but also to conduct experiments aimed at designing systems with intelligence exceeding that of humans. For understandable reasons, they are at an early stage of advancement and are less frequently the subject of research compared to ANI. The research results briefly characterized in this book are classified as ANI.

Among the AGI systems potentially available in the future, Theory of Mind AI (TMAI) systems can be distinguished, which are even supposed to provide the ability to make independent decisions. These decisions are to be made based on processing information in a way very similar to the functioning of the human mind and taking into account emotions, feelings, intentions, motivations, emotional needs, as well as reflecting various types of human thinking and reasoning. This is, to some extent, related to emotion AI, which has been developed for a long time.

It should be mentioned that the most advanced solutions are artificial super intelligence (ASI). Such systems are expected to demonstrate intelligence greater than that of humans when solving many complex cognitive tasks (Song, 2021). ASI will one day achieve the state of self-awareness, have significant cognitive and thinking skills, and understand human emotions and experiences. Perhaps this will be achieved as a result of further development of research related to AGI, and currently such considerations are hypothetical in nature. It is unlikely to be possible to quickly achieve superintelligence, to exceed the point referred to as technological singularity, to reflect the complexity characteristic of the state of the world, to surpass human intelligence in the processes of independent learning and obtaining previously unattainable solutions to problems (Alfonseca et al., 2021).

Self-aware AI (SAAI) is associated with ASI systems. SAAI systems are an idea that is still very far from practical implementation, but the announcements regarding them are very promising and stimulate the imagination. The independence of systems is supposed to mean becoming significantly independent from people and expressing emotional opinions on many important issues. The role of designers and constructors of such systems is mainly limited to computer hardware issues and ends at an early stage, and self-awareness is to eliminate the need to update data and software. The methods of learning and reasoning in SAAI systems, as well as the possibilities of cooperation with people, will be completely different.

For now, classic ANI systems work well in solving inference problems in conditions of uncertainty, that is, when the knowledge describing a specific reality is incomplete and the processed data are not precisely defined or are measured with an accepted margin of error. For example, linguistic information that is difficult to express numerically may be described as uncertain, blurry, or fuzzy.

The considerations presented in this book concern the modeling of a learning system that is based on reasoning under conditions of uncertainty. Empirically acquired knowledge about the evaluated projects is usually incomplete and fuzzy; the processed data is available in various forms and often not precisely defined. In the case of this type of problems, solutions obtained using soft computing methods work well and are very different from conventional hard computing methods operating using strictly defined and unchanging deterministic algorithms.

Soft techniques and technologies useful in constructing computational intelligence systems are often modeled on the functioning of the nervous system and neurons in the human brain. These are systems based on artificial neural networks. Other useful sources of inspiration for the design of AI algorithms may be the theories of evolution and genetics. Inspiration for building intelligent systems may also come from research on mathematical theories, for example, set theory. Among them, solutions related to fuzzy logic applications play an important role. A key feature of such systems is the ability to solve the problem of learning from experimental data by providing a conceptual framework and tools enabling the construction of systems based on empirical knowledge. This knowledge is usually ambiguous, subjective, and imprecise.

The importance and potential capabilities of the previously well-researched ANI systems have been recognized in many fields, including business, finance, e-commerce, healthcare, transportation, education, engineering, physical sciences, and others. Knowledge of AI should therefore not be limited to representatives of technical disciplines of science, technology, engineering, and mathematics (STEM) but also social sciences, business, and management.

AI systems in business are, to put it simply, based on one of the two fundamental concepts: ML and KBS. The most popular ML method is neural networks, often additionally called 'artificial' to distinguish them from natural neurons occurring in the human brain. In turn, the most popular example of KBS is an expert system that relies on human domain expertise.

The most important elements of KBS include knowledge bases, which mainly enable solving decision-making problems related to the selected field of knowledge. The primary role played by knowledge bases is to store the captured knowledge of domain experts. KBS are often based on decision rules generated using, for example, fuzzy logic or rough set theory. There are also known systems constructed on the basis of hybrid techniques combining several selected methods in order to highlight their advantages and minimize the disadvantages of methods used separately.

The beginnings of AI systems are associated with the first work on neural networks, which began at the turn of the 1950s and 1960s. A few years later, as a result of developing generalizations of set theory, fuzzy sets were created (Zadeh, 1965). As part of the development of intelligent systems, research also covered genetic and evolutionary algorithms. In the 1980s (at the Warsaw University of Technology) Professor Zdzisław Pawlak began research on information systems and creating knowledge representations using the rough set theory he invented (Pawlak, 1982, 1991). Research on the development of this theory and its various generalizations has been continued in many centers around the world. The popularity of rough sets (in applications classified as AI) was determined by the ease of implementation of algorithms enabling calculations using objects described with attribute values (criteria), decision rules generation, and knowledge-based decision support (Pawlak, 1997).

The current and future potential of AI does not result from the use of single selected AI models with universal properties. To build effective solutions for organizations, it is necessary to learn a number of concepts, approaches, methods, and tools. Their synthetic overview presented in the following sections is organized according to a simplified classification, which assumes a division into ML and KBS. Neural networks and deep learning are highlighted within ML. In turn, KBS are presented from the point of view of applications of rough sets theory and its generalization useful for knowledge-based decision support in the presence of imprecision, vagueness, and uncertainty. Getting to know these solutions is crucial to understanding the integrated approach and the essence of knowledge-based evaluation.

Machine Learning and Neural Networks

ML is a subset of AI and is based on data-driven learning processes. As experience is gained, while training a selected ML model, dispersed knowledge is accumulated, and this should be accompanied by an improvement in functioning and reduction of errors in the obtained results. The processes of learning and improvement are not deterministic, and their operation is not repeatable – that is, it is not programmed. In ML models, hard computing methods operating using strictly defined and unchangeable algorithms are not applicable. Problems related to the management and evaluation of projects require the use of soft computing methods implemented in intelligent systems that enable obtaining a formal qualitative representation of information and knowledge stored in the form of grains (granules) of information and knowledge.

Intelligent systems have the ability to acquire new knowledge as a result of learning, generalizing the acquired knowledge, and reasoning. They handle empirical data characterized by uncertainty, imprecision, logical inconsistency, and incompleteness. The algorithms used in this type of system often do not have a precise mathematical justification for their correctness. Inspirations for their development are often intuitive or observed in the natural environment surrounding humans.

ML processes identify patterns and correlations in large datasets, which are helpful in supporting decision-making based on forecasting or classification results. The most popular ML methods include neural networks, which are the abstract version of brain cells and were inspired by the results of research on the central nervous system, brain neurons, and the connections between them called synapses. Their operation may be based on various learning paradigms, the most popular of which are the following two types: independent (unsupervised) learning and learning under supervision (supervised). In addition to them, more types of such paradigms are known – for example, semi-supervised learning, transfer learning, positive-unlabeled learning, one-class classification, few/one-shot learning, multi-label learning, and multitask learning (Emmert-Streib et al., 2023). The introduction of subsequent learning concepts is related to the growing number of techniques, methods, and tools useful in ML.

As a result of training the network, the weights assigned to individual connections between neurons arranged in accordance with the previously selected architecture are modified. The topology of neuron connections and the weight values of the trained network are the main elements of models that enable solving desired problems.

The key principles and parameters of network training are mostly selected intuitively. However, attempts are being made to develop theoretical frameworks that are intended to support researchers when looking for answers to questions regarding the selection of types of learning processes, algorithms, and learning conditions necessary to meet them. Such frameworks include probably approximately correct (PAC) and vapnik–chervonenkis (VC) dimension (El Naqa & Chien, 2022). Such ML issues are dealt with by computational learning theory (COLT).

Supervised learning involves searching for the most appropriate network responses (output) in response to input information. For this type of learning, neural networks acquire knowledge based on sets of training examples – that is, sets of input information and the corresponding output information. The networks are then informed about their membership in specific classes or objects, which constitute information from the training set. A decreasing interest in expensive and time-consuming supervised learning with annotated data (labeled manually) can be observed. Only large companies can afford such expensive solutions.

Neural networks are usually resistant to damage and errors occurring in training sets. One can get the correct result from their output even for incomplete and noisy data. On the one hand, they are characterized by enormous application possibilities. It is hard to find a field that has not tried to use them yet. On the other hand, they can undoubtedly be the basis for creating tools and methods with significant capabilities that are easy to use by a wide range of users, even with little IT knowledge. Neural models do not require learning and mathematical description of the relationship between the explanatory (independent) variables and the explained (dependent) variable.

A useful feature of neural networks is their ability for so-called generalization of knowledge – that is, generalization of experience gained in the network learning process. This involves the possibility of generating correct signals at the network outputs, even for input information not previously present in the training set. The disadvantages of neural models undoubtedly include difficulties in justifying and explaining the obtained results. For this reason, trust in such models is usually not high, and the quality of the results obtained largely depends on the experience of network designers.

In addition to neural networks, there are a number of specific areas within biology that can be used as inspiration in the process of developing AI methods. In the case of evolutionary biology, inspirations may be related to modeling on multispecies evolutionary lines, population genetics regarding the formation and development of populations, etc. The operation of evolutionary algorithms, for example, is based on the mechanisms of functioning of a population of individuals (set of acceptable solutions) observed in nature (fighting for survival). Initially, individuals from a given population are randomly selected. Then, one strives to obtain the optimal population by modifying it using evolutionary operators – that is, reproduction, crossing, mutation, and selection. As a result of repeated calculations of this type, a child population is obtained from the parent population, best assessed using the adaptation function adopted (for a given task). Concepts related to evolutionary methods and algorithms include, among others, genetic algorithms, genetic programming, evolution programming, or evolution strategies. However, these types of models are used much less often compared to neural networks, the development of which determines further significant trends in AI.

Important directions of AI development result from the introduction of transformer architecture and the following hybrid forms of learning: self-supervised and semi-supervised. These technologies enable large-scale processing of massive data and obtaining knowledge representations that are adaptable and generalizable. In cases of problems related to project management, there is often a need to prepare a huge amount of labeled data. Labeling a vast training dataset is very time-consuming, long-lasting, and expensive. Semi-supervised learning can function with relatively few labeled data and with large datasets consisting of unlabeled data. The use of self-supervised learning helps reduce this problem by implementing algorithms similar to supervised learning in an unsupervised way.

Models learned using large amounts of unlabeled data by masking certain sections of text, words, sentences, and asking models to fill in those masked sections. This leads to building a powerful representation in the form of language models. Thanks to this, the potential of AI is built to move away from narrow areas of expertise towards broader solutions. Neural networks language models (NNLM) could be trained on huge volumes of unlabeled data coming from, for example, the Internet and acquire natural language skills similar to humans.

If the neural networks are complex and very big (i.e., they consist of many layers with a large number of neurons), the term 'deep' learning is used, which is a significant achievement contributing to the development of subsequent versions of GAI.

Generative AI in Organizations

GAI, which is a recent technological paradigm, enables the processing of large datasets, generating business-useful content, and therefore can be the basis for building an innovative organizational development strategy and contributing to achieving a sustainable competitive advantage. In general, trust in AI technologies is still not high. It is important to make managers of various types of organizations aware of the possibilities resulting from the use of scalable GAI, which can support intelligent analysis of market and business trends, make fast and smart decisions, and use the knowledge to build competitive intelligence strategies thanks to the processing of vast streams of data (Ebrahimi, 2022). GAI can positively influence the improvement of performance and productivity indicators by strengthening dynamic capabilities, increasing competencies, and improving the use of resources (Kombo et al., 2023). Research shows that the competitive rivalry of companies in the field of AI is increasing, and there is a lack of knowledge and skills regarding the effective implementation and scaling of intelligent solutions (Haefner et al., 2023).

GAI, unlike the previously known classic AI, is an innovative AI technology that can be the basis for creating systems that generate new and diverse text and multimedia data. With the help of this technology, it is also possible to conduct a dialogue in natural language thanks to the automatic analysis of content in such a language, identifying the meaning of individual words and phrases and generating personalized answers in a way fully understandable to humans, for example, by virtual assistants. GAI may influence the transformation of previously used IT systems responsible for contacts with customers. The possibilities offered by traditional AI systems are much more limited because they are less flexible in operation and operate according to algorithms that have relatively limited possibilities of modifying and generating a variety of content.

The key to understanding innovative AI technologies and models is to know the relationship between ML (explained in the previous section) and GAI. Within ML, it is possible to distinguish deep learning, which in turn includes discriminative (conditional) models, GAI and LLM.

Most discriminative models function with supervised ML algorithms and are used to solve the problem of classification – that is, determining the boundaries of dividing the data points into different classes. These types of models include, among others, neural networks, logistic regression, decision trees, random forest, and support vector machines.

In turn, much more is expected from GAI, and they are not only used to classify data points. These models are mainly applied to generate new data points using unsupervised ML algorithms. GAI learns about the patterns in the learning datasets, which generates new content – for example, text. GAI models are not intended to solve classification problems or determine exact numerical values. Such models are introduced to generate various types of content – for example, natural languages, texts, or images. The aforementioned content is similar to that used to train these models. Examples of generative models include generative adversarial network (GAN), Bayesian network, autoregressive model, Markov random field, Naive Bayes, and others.

GAI had its beginnings several decades ago but became very popular in 2022, mainly due to the emergence of text-to-image model services and, above all, OpenAI's ChatGPT (Generative Pretrained Transformer) operating in conversational dialogue mode (text-to-text). One can also find other solutions involving generating images or video based on text (text-to-image or text-to-video). Solutions classified as LLM Chatbots (e.g., ChatGPT or Google Bard) can be located in the common part of two following sets: GAI and LLM (Figure 2.1).

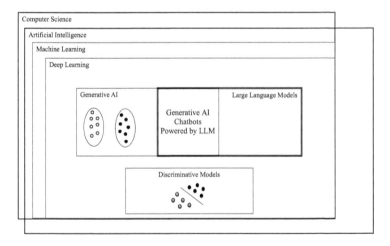

Figure 2.1 Relations between ML, GAI, and chatbots powered by LLM

Source: Inspired by (Banh & Strobel, 2023; Jebara, 2003)

AI is based on interdisciplinary research and is largely a part of computer science. However, these fields are not entirely related. There are a number of studies that cannot be classified as computer science because they are related to selected fields of social sciences – for example, psychology and cognitive science. Of course, there is also a lot of research in computer science that is not classified as AI.

GAI models are based on achievements in the fields of neural networks and deep learning. The term 'generative' is related to creating new content (text, images, audio, video, or even computer code) by analyzing information and patterns from training data. GAI uses language modeling and LLM, which are the basis for developing innovative ways of representing language, used to solve natural language processing (NLP) tasks and based on large sets of text data. The use of language modeling and natural language generation systems enables the creation of solutions allowing for natural language understanding, translation of sequences of words in some context, text generation, and question answering. NNLM therefore make it possible to support the prediction of answers to specific questions that are sequences of words in some contexts.

GAI is based on a certain architecture of an intelligent system, principles of computer calculations, and large sets of empirical data. Using the adopted method of data analysis, it is possible to discover relationships and predict sequences to create new knowledge that is made available in various forms, such as text, images, audio, video, and others. In order to improve model performance and the ability to generate artificial data using GAI, transfer learning is used. This type of learning may additionally help solve the problem of limited data in ML, NLP, computer vision, and computer graphics (Park et al., 2023; Wang et al., 2023).

GAI, LLM, and transfer learning can play a key role in organizations and be the basis for building effective tools for improving business operations, optimizing processes, and supporting increasing creativity and innovation. Examples of such applications include the following:

1. Enhancing sustainability in IT management by improving energy efficiency, refining sustainable resource management, and sustainable design and development in the IT industry (Ooi et al., 2023).
2. Boosting creativity, generating new ideas, and facilitating the creation of new designs in product and services design processes (Pagani & Champion, 2023a).
3. Automating tasks that are highly structured and manual, redesigning work processes, and other changes in the workplace (Ooi et al., 2023).
4. Strengthening effective organizational collaboration and facilitating communications enable easier generation of creative solutions (Dencik et al., 2023; Gamoura et al., 2024; Walkowiak, 2023).

5. Augmenting digital prototyping and improving work during early phases of innovation thanks to the use of GPT, which is a representative of the LLM set (Bilgram & Laarmann, 2023).
6. Optimizing processes, increasing efficiency and productivity by automating simple tasks and offering time for employees to perform unique, complex, and innovative tasks (Pagani & Champion, 2023b).

Rough Set Models

It is advisable to integrate the GAI discussed in the previous section with traditional AI models. Among these solutions with great potential are rough set models (based on rough set theory), which are useful in building learning systems that can be used to solve many practical problems related to, for example, data analysis and classifying various types of objects. Models of this type are used for management problems that cannot be described using deterministic mathematical models. Such models are based on the unrealistic assumption of the deterministic nature of the analyzed socioeconomic processes – that is, that they are clearly and precisely defined and that there are only objectively verifiable factors.

The relationships resulting from rough set theory can be successfully used to model systems based on empirical knowledge, which is usually ambiguous, subjective, and imprecise. The applications of this theory may be analogous to the possibilities of previously known fuzzy logic modeling and its use in solving problems with learning from experimental data. Rough set models have found many applications related to decision support in management, engineering, and industry due to their practical usefulness and flexibility (Peters et al., 2012; Sangaiah et al., 2016).

The functioning of rough set models is inspired by the human way of thinking, which is certainly much less precise than calculations using deterministic computer algorithms. For example, the terms 'small' and 'large' are unclear for such algorithms. For calculations and comparative analyses using deterministic models, precisely defined dimensions with specified accuracy are necessary. The great usefulness of rough set models and similar fuzzy systems results from their low precision in analyzing phenomena, in a way comparable to people's use of uncertain knowledge and expressing imprecise opinions about the surrounding reality.

Rough set models can be the basis for designing AI systems whose functioning is grounded in inspirations resulting from the modification of classical mathematics and an interesting development of classical set theory. Modifications of classical mathematical instruments are necessary when solving problems related to empirical data, for example, in assessed projects. Classical set theory and two-valued logic are then most often of little use.

When solving many practical problems, it is desirable to use soft extensions and generalizations of set theory that accept gradations of values and unclear assignments of objects to specific sets. These types of approaches are known primarily in two sister theories: fuzzy set theory and rough set theory. These theories provide tools for reasoning under conditions of uncertainty, as well as for analyzing uncertain, blurry, fuzzy, or incomplete data.

Fuzzy set theory assumes that objects can only partially belong to specific sets. In the case of analysis carried out using only classical set theory, objects may either belong or not belong to defined sets. Rough set theory is the result of research on the logical features of an information board containing a description of objects occurring in the analyzed reality. According to this theory, a fuzzy concept can be represented as two sharp concepts, called lower and upper approximations. Rough set theory allows you to process empirically obtained data, similarly to fuzzy set theory. However, the theory presented in this section is not as popular, to some extent, as complementary fuzzy set theory.

In many respects, rough set models may be more useful in practice than fuzzy set models in work on creating knowledge bases in certain selected, narrow fields – in knowledge-intensive, domain-specific learning processes. Moreover, fuzzy set algorithms are more difficult to analyze than those based on rough sets. In the case of the latter, there is no need for preliminary assumptions regarding the dependencies between attributes, which are necessary in calculations using fuzzy sets. In the case of fuzzy modeling, it is also relatively difficult to generate decision rules and build systems with rule-based knowledge bases. Fuzzy sets require the use of complex fuzzification and defuzzification procedures for calculations, which involve large computational costs and may sometimes cause significant errors when conducting data analyses. The advantages of rough set models determine their selection for use as one of the most important elements in the AI-driven knowledge-based evaluation system (described in more detail in Chapter 4).

Knowledge-Based Systems

KBS are a subdiscipline of AI related to knowledge discovery and representation. Quantitative and qualitative knowledge obtained from various sources can be transformed into a form that allows it to be saved, processed, and used. Appropriate selection of the knowledge representation method ensures access to it with selected tools and its subsequent use with reasoning mechanisms. KBS are primarily RBS and use knowledge-driven rules to support decisions. Practical aspects of the implementation and operation of this type of system are dealt with, among others, by knowledge engineering, which is closely related to the concepts of software engineering, information engineering, and information systems engineering.

The development of KBS runs in parallel with research on classic IT systems that use databases and data warehouses instead of knowledge bases. A database is a set of data saved in accordance with an adopted data model (data representation) and software (a set of programs) constituting a database management system (DBMS) that manages access to data and also enables reading, saving, and modifying it. In order to emphasize the relationship between databases and technologies for representing and discovering knowledge, the concept of Knowledge Discovery in Databases was introduced.

Organizations usually face the problem of having to integrate data from multiple databases and various types of external sources. Additionally, conditions should be created for data mining. It is also necessary to implement various types of decision support systems that search, analyze, and present data as part of online analytical processing (OLAP). All this has led to the creation of a special type of databases called data warehouses, which are the basic elements of Business Intelligence systems used in organizations to collect and provide knowledge supporting decision-making processes.

Unlike databases and data warehouses, knowledge bases not only enable building information structures, but were also created as a result of the evolution of classic database concepts, which were supplemented with inference mechanisms (i.e., drawing conclusions based on knowledge resulting from data). Knowledge bases constitute a record of the knowledge of specialists in a given field, understood as information that has been given a specific structure in order to enable its use in a certain context and in a selected field.

In addition to classic databases and knowledge bases, there are also intermediate solutions. These include, for example, deductive database, whose characteristic feature is the ability to deduce new data based on previously recorded information. This database usually consists of two databases (subsystems), one of which is used for classic data storage in accordance with the adopted data model. The second database contains written inference rules according to which the process of deduction of new data is carried out. These types of databases have a principle of operation similar to that of expert systems. KBS are a more general concept compared to expert systems. In the case of KBS, the importance of system architecture and the central role of the knowledge base are emphasized. Expert systems are KBS for which it is important to carry out tasks related to expert knowledge workers in organizations.

An expert system usually consists of a knowledge base, inference rules, and, most often, a multimedia interface for contacts with the system user. The knowledge base contains constant knowledge and variable knowledge that relates to the current situation, problem, etc. In addition, the database contains a set of inference rules. Expert systems use stored knowledge (on a given topic) to solve problems and make decisions that usually require the participation of a human expert. Systems with a knowledge base most often perform advisory functions (decisions are then made by humans) or, less frequently, decision-making functions, and they formulate decisions without human participation and implement them. Other types of expert systems include criticizing (commenting on proposed solutions), diagnostic (evaluating an object or process), and instructional (supporting the teaching process).

Among the abovementioned types of KBS and expert systems, the idea of very advanced and increasingly autonomous inclusion of KBS in corporate governance arouses great interest in the world of science and business practice. Particularly interesting is a preliminary legal analysis and comparison of the management of traditional corporations, leaderless or memberless entities. Important issues are related to delegating selected decision-making rights to AI or even full replacement of human directors by KBS and assigning responsibility for errors made by artificial AI systems (Mertens, 2023).

Constructing a KBS model requires an interdisciplinary approach covering issues related to various technologies. In addition to issues concerning databases, knowledge bases, and methods of processing uncertain information, it is necessary to use the previously mentioned ML. KBS can be implemented in various ways, but systems with rule-based knowledge bases deserve special attention. In this type of system, reasoning involves drawing conclusions based on knowledge recorded in the form of rules and using a selected method.

There are two basic methods of reasoning: deductive and inductive, which may, for example, be based on empirical examples. Inductive reasoning can lead to generalizations as a result of the analysis of known objects, which are combined into specific sets, created in terms of having certain common features. In turn, deductive reasoning involves formulating conclusions based on facts resulting from knowledge stored in the database in the form of rules. These conclusions are considered valid if an assumption is made about the correctness of the decision rules.

Generally speaking, the use of a learning system and building a knowledge base can take place in two stages: inducing decision rules and searching for decision rules enabling the desired classification. The first stage of rule induction is performed on the basis of examples learned from the system, which is characterized by a set of conditional and decision-making attributes. In the case of project classification, one decision attribute is used. In the second stage, decision rules for new and unclassified objects are sought to enable their assignment to specific subsets known as decision classes.

Decision rules can be generated from examples – that is, training objects with known classifications. These rules are intended to be used to classify new objects. In other words, decision rules define decision classes for new objects – they are their classifiers. Some object evaluation processes may involve assigning new objects, described using evaluation criteria, to one of the decision classes. The existence of these classes is established a priori, that is, by assumption. As a result of the so-called sorting objects constituting previously evaluated objects, they are assigned to individual classes, which are, for example, ordered according to the principle of dominance.

Taking into account the psychological aspect of evaluation, it is possible to study the system that organizes the intellectual processes taking place in the minds of experts evaluating projects. The system of intellectual activities, attitudes, and competences shapes the essence of human actions and the decisions they make. Human decision-making thinking can be presented in the form of a decision table containing individual decision options and the criteria for their evaluation. The instrument used to select one of the variants (considered the most advantageous) is a decision rule. One of the ways to organize decision-making thinking is dominance search, often utilized by managers. Another method is to use the so-called natural decision rules that reflect the spontaneous thought processes of decision-makers leading to making specific decisions.

In the form of decision rules, incomplete and general knowledge, referred to as heuristic knowledge, can be represented. It is a record of experts' experience gathered in the process of solving a given problem in a particular field – for example, selected decision-making problems and previous classification of objects. Heuristic rules can be used to support decision-making related to various types of partial and comprehensive problems in the field of project management. The increasing importance of these types of applications results from the dynamic development of the so-called agile (adaptive, light) project management methodologies, that is, Agile Project Management consistent with the Agile Principles recorded in the so-called Agile Manifesto. The author of this book conducted theoretical and practical research using heuristic rules generated based on empirical data to build knowledge bases and use them in a flexible and adaptive project evaluation system (Grzeszczyk, 2012).

The rule-based and symbolic representation of knowledge used in many intelligent systems allows for further direct use by humans or in the process of automated classification. The constructed set of rules should contribute to the creation of an inference schema, which is then used to support decision-making. The logical form of the decision rule is as follows:

IF {set of conditional attributes specifying the fulfillment of specific conditions} THEN {the decision resulting from the fulfillment of these conditions}.

The decision rule therefore consists of two parts: conditional and decision. The first of these parts is the premises for making a specific decision. It is built in the form of a conjunction or alternative of conditional attributes describing objects. The second part specifies the conclusion and determines its assignment to a specific decision class. Due to the fact that the conditional and decision parts of a decision rule are analyzed as logical values taking two values – true or false – decision rules are called predicates, and the processing of rules is called predicate calculus.

Thus, the term 'rule system' refers to decision rules. For completeness, it is worth mentioning another class of rules that are often the subject of research, the so-called association rules. Unlike decision rules, they only reflect the dependencies between the conditional attributes appearing in the premise of the decision rule. Association rule-generation algorithms do not analyze concepts related to decision classes.

Decision rules are one of the most popular knowledge representation methods due to their transparent nature, application possibilities, and advantages, which include the following:

1. A clear and understandable way of representing knowledge in the form of an IF-THEN statement containing a condition and a prediction.
2. A uniform and symbolic record of specialized and interdisciplinary knowledge in a specific field.
3. Clear interpretation of the obtained result (e.g., classification) based on simple decision rules.
4. Processing empirically obtained qualitative information that is impossible or difficult to analyze using other methods.
5. Relatively easy reasoning mechanisms functioning in a human-like manner – as opposed to complex numerical algorithms.
6. Susceptibility to system scalability, if necessary, to expand the knowledge base – by adding new rules.
7. A simple solution to specific classification problems is to select a particular subset from the total set of decision rules.
8. The relative ease of implementing the system as a practically helpful application with a graphical user interface enables data entry and knowledge acquisition.

In many modern decision-making processes, a key role is played by empirically obtained data, which are usually characterized by inconsistencies resulting from the granularity of information, inaccuracy, incompleteness, uncertainty, and ambiguity of the description of the analyzed socioeconomic phenomena. Using KBS to solve complex problems makes it possible to consider factors omitted in the case of deterministic systems and classic statistical methods, that is, deemed erroneous and impossible to analyze.

Using a rule-based knowledge base approach enables obtaining an easy-to-interpret representation of preferences and discovering principles and mechanisms of decision-making based on complex and unstructured data for which specific data models are missing. Great hopes can be placed on developing KBS and integrating these systems with GAI solutions, which can accelerate, facilitate, and automate multicriteria decision-making in various organizations.

References

Alfonseca, M., Cebrian, M., Fernandez Anta, A., Coviello, L., Abeliuk, A., & Rahwan, I. (2021). Superintelligence cannot be contained: Lessons from computability theory. *Journal of Artificial Intelligence Research, 70,* 65–76. https://doi.org/10.1613/jair.1.12202

Banh, L., & Strobel, G. (2023). Generative artificial intelligence. *Electronic Markets, 33*(1), 63. https://doi.org/10.1007/s12525-023-00680-1

Bilgram, V., & Laarmann, F. (2023). Accelerating innovation with genera-tive AI: AI-augmented digital prototyping and innovation methods. *IEEE Engineering Management Review*, *51*(2), 18–25. https://doi.org/10.1109/EMR.2023.3272799

Dencik, J., Goehring, B., & Marshall, A. (2023). Managing the emerging role of generative AI in next-generation business. *Strategy and Leadership*, *51*(6), 30–36. https://doi.org/10.1108/SL-08-2023-0079

Ebrahimi, M. (2022). Development of competitive intelligence to formulate business strategy using emerging technologies: Deployment of artificial intel-ligence. In H. Taherdoost (Ed.), *Advances in e-business research* (pp. 124–143). IGI Global. https://doi.org/10.4018/978-1-6684-5235-6.ch006

El Naqa, I., & Chien, J.-T. (2022). Computational learning theory. In I. El Naqa & M. J. Murphy (Eds.), *Machine and deep learning in oncology, medical physics and radiology* (pp. 17–26). Springer International Publish-ing. https://doi.org/10.1007/978-3-030-83047-2_2

Emmert-Streib, F., Moutari, S., & Dehmer, M. (2023). Foundations of learn-ing from data. In F. Emmert-Streib, S. Moutari, & M. Dehmer (Eds.), *Elements of data science, machine learning, and artificial intelligence using R* (pp. 489–520). Springer International Publishing. https://doi.org/10.1007/978-3-031-13339-8_17

Gamoura, S. C., Koruca, H. İ., & Urgancı, K. B. (2024). Exploring the tran-sition from "contextual AI" to "generative AI" in management: Cases of ChatGPT and DALL-E 2. In Z. Şen, Ö. Uygun, & C. Erden (Eds.), *Advances in intelligent manufacturing and service system informatics* (pp. 368–381). Springer Nature Singapore. https://doi.org/10.1007/978-981-99-6062-0_34

Grzeszczyk, T. A. (2012). *Modelling evaluation of European projects*. Placet (In Polish).

Haefner, N., Parida, V., Gassmann, O., & Wincent, J. (2023). Implement-ing and scaling artificial intelligence: A review, framework, and research agenda. *Technological Forecasting and Social Change*, *197*, 122878. https://doi.org/10.1016/j.techfore.2023.122878

Jebara, T. (2003). *Machine learning: Discriminative and generative* (2004th ed.). Springer.

Kim, J., Lee, S., & Seong, P. H. (2023). Artificial intelligence and methods. In J. Kim, S. Lee, & P. H. Seong (Eds.), *Autonomous nuclear power plants with artificial intelligence* (Vol. 94, pp. 9–28). Springer International Pub-lishing. https://doi.org/10.1007/978-3-031-22386-0_2

Kombo, V., Asbaş, C., & Tuzlukaya, Ş. E. (2023). Artificial intelligence, dynamic capabilities, and business optimization: Impact on firm per-formance. In M. Hernández Hernández (Ed.), *Advances in business information systems and analytics* (pp. 1–20). IGI Global. https://doi.org/10.4018/978-1-6684-8639-9.ch001

McLean, S., Read, G. J. M., Thompson, J., Baber, C., Stanton, N. A., & Salmon, P. M. (2023). The risks associated with Artificial General Intelligence: A systematic review. *Journal of Experimental & Theoretical Artificial Intel-ligence*, *35*(5), 649–663. https://doi.org/10.1080/0952813X.2021.1964003

Mertens, F. (2023). The use of artificial intelligence in corporate decision-making at board level: A preliminary legal analysis. *SSRN Electronic Jour-nal*. https://doi.org/10.2139/ssrn.4339413

Ooi, K.-B., Tan, G. W.-H., Al-Emran, M., Al-Sharafi, M. A., Capatina, A., Chakraborty, A., Dwivedi, Y. K., Huang, T.-L., Kar, A. K., Lee, V.-H., Loh, X.-M., Micu, A., Mikalef, P., Mogaji, E., Pandey, N., Raman, R., Rana, N. P., Sarker, P., Sharma, A., . . . Wong, L.-W. (2023). The potential of generative artificial intelligence across disciplines: Perspectives and future directions. *Journal of Computer Information Systems*. https://doi.org/10.1080/0887441 7.2023.2261010

Pagani, M., & Champion, R. (2023a). *Artificial intelligence for business creativity* (p. 137). Routledge. https://doi.org/10.4324/9781003287582

Pagani, M., & Champion, R. (2023b). How AI can foster business creativity. In *Artificial intelligence for business creativity* (pp. 65–81). Routledge https://doi.org/10.4324/9781003287582-7

Park, S.-W., Kim, J.-Y., Park, J., Jung, S.-H., & Sim, C.-B. (2023). How to train your pre-trained GAN models. *Applied Intelligence*, *53*(22), 27001–27026. https://doi.org/10.1007/s10489-023-04807-x

Pawlak, Z. (1982). Rough sets. *International Journal of Computer and Information Sciences*, *11*, 341–356.

Pawlak, Z. (1991). *Rough sets: Theoretical aspects of reasoning about data* (1991st ed.). Kluwer Academic Publishers.

Pawlak, Z. (1997). Rough set approach to knowledge-based decision support. *European Journal of Operational Research*, *99*(1), 48–57. https://doi.org/10.1016/S0377-2217(96)00382-7

Peters, G., Lingras, P., Ślęzak, D., & Yao, Y. (Eds.). (2012). *Rough sets: Selected methods and applications in management and engineering* (2012th ed.). Springer.

Sangaiah, A. K., Gao, X.-Z., & Abraham, A. (Eds.). (2016). *Handbook of research on fuzzy and rough set theory in organizational decision making* (1st ed.). Business Science Reference.

Sifakis, J., & Harel, D. (2023). Trustworthy autonomous system development. *ACM Transactions on Embedded Computing Systems*, *22*(3), 1–24. https://doi.org/10.1145/3545178

Song, B. (Ed.). (2021). *Intelligence and wisdom: Artificial intelligence meets Chinese philosophers*. Springer Nature Singapore. https://doi.org/10.1007/978-981-16-2309-7

Walkowiak, E. (2023). Task-interdependencies between Generative AI and Workers. *Economics Letters*, *231*, 111315. https://doi.org/10.1016/j.econlet.2023.111315

Wang, B., Kato, S., & Kano, M. (2023). GAN-based homogenous transfer learning method for regression problems. *2023 IEEE conference on control technology and applications (CCTA)* (pp. 85–90). https://doi.org/10.1109/CCTA54093.2023.10252827

Zadeh, L. A. (1965). Fuzzy sets. *Information and Control*, *8*(3), 338–353. https://doi.org/10.1016/S0019-9958(65)90241-X

3 Selected AI Applications in Project Management

Data-Driven Project Management

The field of project management is constantly changing due to widely noticeable progress in data science and emerging disruptive new AI technologies. Data plays a key role in the context of all types of ICT systems, but in the case of AI algorithms, the demands on empirical data used in, for example, ML are particularly high. Data should be collected in accordance with business ethics, and AI models should be trained on legally obtained data of acceptable quality. Data ought to be free of bias, hate speech, and toxic elements. It is also necessary to formulate recommendations regarding the need not only to improve datasets and the AI models used but also to build trust in the decisions and recommendations provided by newer versions of AI.

Data-driven project managers should deal with difficulties related to data, its diversity, and ensuring its appropriate quality. Data-driven project management is a developing field in the discipline of management sciences that concerns the correct use of empirical project data and implementation analytics to make informed decisions supporting the improvement of project outcomes and long-term benefits.

In today's reality, ensuring the integration of project management, as well as data, information and knowledge management plays a key role. AI and data science achievements are increasingly used in projects. The following tools and instruments supporting information and knowledge management are particularly important:

1. Collecting data and documenting knowledge using simple office applications: word processors, spreadsheets, presentation development programs, and small DBMS.
2. IT systems of varying complexity and functionality that support project management by facilitating the development of schedules, as well as managing budget, staff, risk, communication, and others.
3. Groupware systems that support workflow and interactivity within cooperation in the processes of carrying out design and evaluation tasks.

DOI: 10.4324/9781003341611-3

4. Repository of data and knowledge available in centralized and distributed forms – peer-to-peer, local repositories related to individual members of the project team, between whom knowledge is exchanged.
5. Decision support systems with model databases, which are used to develop simulation models of planned projects.
6. Data warehouse enabling the identification of goals at individual management levels, controlling their implementation, generating reports, comparative statements, simulations and forecasts in cooperation with Online Transaction Processing technologies, multidimensional OLAP, and data mining technologies.
7. Knowledge maps based on the technique of memory maps and mind mapping, which support the creation of strategic knowledge resources, structuring of project knowledge, visualization of concepts, etc.
8. Project intelligence systems that can support the simulation of projects and the analysis of their risk factors using more advanced technologies, for example, KBS, Business Intelligence systems, and expert systems.
9. Knowledge bases containing facts and rules in a specific field obtained from experts.
10. Systems supporting the search for experts that enable the management of knowledge about human potential.
11. Human Resource Management Systems supporting the discovery of field specialists useful for implementing specific projects.
12. E-learning systems supporting the transfer of design knowledge at a distance as part of distance education (distance learning) using two modes: synchronous, when the participants of the educational process and the instructors are active at the same time (videoconferencing, web conferencing); asynchronous, when data, information, and didactic knowledge are delivered and reproduced at different times.
13. Exchange of data and knowledge via an intranet or extranet understood as a connection of several intranets (internal networks of organizations based on Internet technologies).
14. Exchange of data and knowledge within corporate portals and knowledge portals (e.g., vertical portals) that operate on intranets, extranets, or the Internet.

Data-driven project managers can use the following systems to discover knowledge from data and manage domain knowledge:

1. Intelligent systems based on AI methods that are used to extract knowledge from large sets of unstructured data and discover relationships in data.
2. KBS implementing automatic inference and gathering knowledge in a formalized form for decision-support purposes.
3. Knowledge repositories and databases enabling the exchange and distribution of knowledge from domain experts.

4. Multimedia systems collecting experience from previous projects, which can be the basis for building repositories of knowledge potentially useful to support solving current design problems.
5. Conversational AI, which, using interactive systems, enables the accumulation of knowledge through a human-machine dialogue.
6. GAI systems that enable the generation of knowledge in various forms, including text, images, and videos.

Project managers should use not only concepts and methods known from the social sciences and management. It is necessary to open up to new interdisciplinary approaches and intelligent data and design knowledge management systems that are based on computational technologies known from the exact sciences: mathematics, logic, and computer science.

The importance of data, information, and knowledge in the field of project management is similar to the other fields within the discipline of management science. The difficulties associated with the use of project data include, on the one hand, the availability of data of appropriate quality, and on the other hand, coping with the analysis of huge available datasets, sometimes of low quality, so that it contributes to improving decision-making, for example, as part of integrated project management and control. One example of a concept consistent with data-driven project management may be the construction of an integrated framework for project management and control consisting of the following three components: schedule risk analysis, baseline scheduling, and project control (Vanhoucke, 2023b).

Project managers need empirical data for, among others, periodic collection and monitoring of progress in project implementation and evaluation of current project performance indicators. In addition to project managers, academic researchers also need access to this data to conduct experiments with newly developed analytics methods. Without access to empirical project data, researchers often create hypothetical projects to study and validate new methods. However, first of all, actual empirical data should be available for scientific research, because this allows for the study to be carried out that provides truly practically useful results taking into account many of the strengths and weaknesses of the analyzed phenomena (Vanhoucke, 2023a).

AI technology skills are currently playing a key role in the competitive race for project managers who can stand out by having this type of knowledge. In order to become data-driven project managers, they should have not only key nontechnical skills but also the technical skills and competencies required in connection with the needs related to the applications of AI technology. As shown by the conducted research, for projects characterized by significant socio-technical complexity, the core competence of project managers is leadership, while the most important dimension of this competence is project management knowledge (Ahmadi Eftekhari et al., 2022). The results of other surveys indicate that communication, commitment, and leadership are project managers' core competencies crucial to achieving project success (Alvarenga et al., 2019).

Data-driven project managers should combine key nontechnical and digital skills necessary to implement, among others, dynamic scheduling and data analytics. Conscious decision-making by these managers also requires knowledge of statistical data analysis methods and techniques, as well as data gathering procedures and statistical software.

Nowadays, having digital skills is as important as classic knowledge of project management. Improving these types of skills is an essential requirement for project managers to succeed in a volatile and changing environment (Marhraoui, 2023). Acceptance of innovative AI technologies and, in particular, possession of GAI-related skills is desirable and positively distinguishes project managers.

Generative AI in Modern Project Management

In computer sciences and AI technologies, there is constant progress and the emergence of new advanced ML and GAI solutions, which is a new challenge for project management. It is worth exploring the world of GAI and discovering its potential chances related to project management carried out with engaged stakeholders and more effective activities aimed at project success. The emergence of this technology means revolutionary changes and opportunities that can be used by conscious data-driven project managers, for example, in analyzing stakeholders and improving communication with them, refining cooperation in project teams, automating simple activities and tasks, and improving decision-making based on knowledge discovered from data.

GAI started its triumphal march towards success relatively recently (in late 2022), but a large number of solutions useful in business can already be noticed. In the field of project management, there are still relatively few of them, and therefore GAI's significant potential possibilities have not been sufficiently discovered, not only in providing knowledge necessary to improve existing processes but above all in generating new, creative content that facilitates obtaining the desired results.

The available solutions include, for example, the ability to design and implement intelligent, efficient work processes. When mapped, they can be improved to reduce human involvement in the implementation of routine tasks through digital transformation and automation of some of the processes. It is possible to support the integration of interdependent processes and significantly improve the workflow, make it easier for teams to monitor and coordinate project activities, improve the administration of repetitive tasks, analyze data on an ongoing basis, and track project performance values (Salleh & Aziz, 2022). The time saved in this way can be spent on more ambitious tasks and focusing on strategic aspects of projects.

Another potential application area for GAI is project planning, although AI-generated project plans are often imperfect and should still be checked and manually corrected by humans. This is confirmed by the results of comparative analyses of the content and structure of plans generated with the support of GAI and the plans developed by project managers. The use of independently functioning GAI in project management, especially in planning processes, does not ensure sufficient effectiveness in obtaining the correct and desired results. For now, it is most appropriate to develop plans as a result of the joint work of GAI systems and managers (Barcaui & Monat, 2023).

One of the advantages of AI resulting from the nature of many such models is the ability to learn based on historical project data and forecast resource requirements or generate different variants of project schedules. It is also possible to facilitate project planning by generating alternative scenarios for implementing the activities leading to diverse project outcomes.

With the support of GAI, it is also possible to generate problem trees in the process of planning and defining projects, as well as identifying potential risks and possible bottlenecks. After transforming the generated problem trees into goal trees, GAI can help analyze, evaluate, and select one of the possible variants of the strategy for implementing selected projects and programs.

GAI can help engage stakeholders in project implementation with features that facilitate NLP communication. It is therefore possible to support communication, which is crucial for stakeholder management and the effective work of project teams. Individual team members can use generated personalized recommendations and task assignments adequate to their functions and planned tasks to be performed. Thanks to the ability to generate alternative project implementation scenarios and predict possible difficulties, it is also possible to identify the risks and at the same time indicate mitigation strategies that allow solving potential problems.

Significant benefits are also available when using GAI to support work with design approaches and tools used in the Architecture, Engineering, and Construction sector. Such supported and newly developed approaches include, for example, Computer-Aided Design and Building Information Modeling. Preliminary research results on the applications of GAI in this type of field are promising, but attention is drawn to the difficulties with the still necessary high involvement of people in the entire process of developing designs and the need to solve complex problems related to the often large number of generated alternative solutions (Oscar et al., 2023).

Another interesting application of GAI is in the field of software development, because it has the potential to increase software engineering productivity. This is due to the possibility of automatic code generation, independent work by GAI systems during software development processes, and support for customer feedback analysis (Oscar et al., 2023).

AI should be looked at not from the perspective of something unique, unusual, and distinctive of the projects using it but above all as the value it adds to these projects (Odeh, 2023). Tools supporting project management using GAI can have a positive impact on the efficiency of undertaken activities, formulating effective strategies and identifying potential risks thanks to the implementation of predictive analytics that takes into account historical data on projects, team performance indicators, and factors related to external conditions and the demand for necessary resources. GAI can be the basis for creating effective tools supporting project monitoring in real time and correcting the distribution of resources in order to dynamically adapt them to the changing project environment and the resulting needs.

GAI chatbots can effectively support tracing/tracking project processes, risk and resource management, as well as schedule and cost analysis (Taboada et al., 2023). It can be noted that increasingly advanced applications of innovative AI technologies are useful in improving project management procedures in accordance with contemporary requirements, needs, and selected standards and methodologies, for example, the Project Management Body of Knowledge (Hashfi & Raharjo, 2023).

Learning Models for Project Evaluation

Evaluation plays a key role in learning from success and failure, acquiring knowledge useful in periodic decision-making, and also contributing to conscious monitoring and the ongoing selection of one of the possible methods of action in project management. Thanks to properly conducted evaluation, it is possible to influence the following three functions: control, management, and learning. To ensure the effectiveness of these functions, it is necessary to choose various methods of data collection and analysis, which should be selected adequately to different evaluation criteria (Samset & Volden, 2022). This differentiation of criteria lies in the existence of quantitative and qualitative evaluation measures, which are particularly difficult to take into account, especially in complex project situations (Thamhain, 2013). It is therefore necessary to select often complex multicriteria evaluation models (Azevedo De Souza et al., 2022). Models enabling comprehensive project evaluation also include mixed intelligent systems based on quantitative and qualitative methods (Grzeszczyk, 2018).

Various project evaluation models can be used to analyze the past and current effects of activities or to forecast them. The main role of these models is to support rational decision-making, which should lead to solving the existing problems and achieving the assumed goals. Among many, there are symbolic models, which use symbols such as drawings, charts, as well as entries with specific mathematical symbols, decision rules, and others.

A given section of reality can be characterized using the language of mathematical modeling and building mathematical models. They are a set of symbols and mathematical relations describing the modeled fragment of reality. It is necessary to ensure that the selected mathematical tools resulting from the adopted approach to solving the research problem are compatible with the symbols and mathematical relations that constitute the model. A set of chosen mathematical objects creates a certain mathematical structure that can be described as a system.

Mathematical models use formalized concepts, structures, mathematical language and are only simplified descriptions of real systems or selected aspects of their operation. When building evaluation models, it is possible to use interdisciplinary modeling principles known from operational research and decision theory. Among the operational research models, taking into account the classification related to solution search methods, three types can be distinguished: analytical, simulation, and heuristic. The first one is based on a formalized mathematical description used to search for solutions close to optimal, while the second one usually uses complex simulation algorithms.

In the case of heuristic models, certain general principles are used that approximately describe the analyzed phenomena. Heuristic models prove to be valuable in situations where it is difficult to find solutions considered close to optimal using analytical and simulation models. Such situations occur in decision-making problems regarding new and unique projects characterized by multi-aspect goals, the implementation of which is assessed with measurable and nonmeasurable criteria (described qualitatively).

In the past, most mathematical models were deterministic, where inputs and precisely defined values were clearly assigned specific output states. However, models of this type have many limitations and do not take into account the random phenomena and uncertainties typical of the real world. They are only good for solving well-defined problems. Over time, nondeterministic solution models began to be developed – that is, stochastic and probabilistic ones based on stochastic processes – in which the model states are determined only with a certain probability.

Another useful direction in the development of nondeterministic decision models is provided by the previously mentioned fuzzy sets and their sister theory, rough sets. Both approaches extend the possibilities of classical set theory. These approaches are to some extent consistent with cognitive decision theory, and it is possible to use them to solve evaluation problems that are usually unstructured and imprecisely defined qualitatively in a way typical of many problems that usually occur in reality.

The increasing usefulness of nondeterministic decision models results from the persistent tendency of destabilization and increasing uncertainty of the environment, and it is not possible to effectively deterministically model phenomena in conditions of increasing risk and uncertainty, unpredictable changes, turbulence, unexpected crises, and fluctuations. These features of the environment increase the need to use nondeterministic learning models in evaluation. Continuous learning and quick action in response to changes in the environment are crucial.

An additional argument for the need to use nondeterministic learning models is the increasing importance of qualitative, unstructured, vague, and imprecisely defined decision-making problems related to the evaluation of projects characterized by significant risk and uncertainty. Symbolic methods based on computer learning algorithms may be useful when solving classification problems related to project evaluation. These methods can provide a clear form of knowledge representation, a heuristic nature, and interdisciplinary quality measures particularly useful for conducting multifaceted evaluations. Methods based on symbolic representation of knowledge can be developed using selected mathematical instruments and new AI technologies.

Nondeterministic learning models turn out to be useful when changes are becoming increasingly complex and occurring faster. In these conditions, it is necessary to move away from linear and quantitative attempts to describe the complex, multidimensional, and turbulent reality. Holistic and iterative models with a nonlinear feedback loop should be built, taking into account the dynamics of changes taking place, and models based only on simple and short cause-and-effect chains should be rejected. It is crucial to focus on evaluation research on multilateral and multi-aspect connections in the modeled systems.

The accumulation and static use of knowledge resources are insufficient, and therefore it is necessary to take into account the effects resulting from non-linear feedback and updating knowledge adequately to current circumstances. Consideration of dynamic dependencies is possible by recording knowledge in the form of rules of conduct reflecting the behavior of the evaluated projects and their relations with the environment.

By implementing a continuous learning process, iterative and permanent improvement of the evaluation system can be ensured, which can situationally adapt to specific and variable phenomena. The issues of continuous learning and model improvement are present in many modern management concepts such as Total Quality Management, Kaizen, Continuous Improvement Theory, as well as quality circles, that is, continuous improvement in accordance with the Deming Plan-Do-Check-Act cycle, also known as Plan-Do-Study-Act. These processes of continuous learning and improvement can be supported by AI methods.

Taking into account the above comments, the following recommendations can be made regarding learning models in project evaluation:

1. A multi-aspect approach to the project evaluation process should be made, allowing for the consideration of various quantitative and qualitative evaluation criteria regarding economic, social, environmental, legal, and other aspects.
2. It is necessary to ensure the possibility of conducting evaluation in accordance with the adopted principles, measures and standards.
3. The developed evaluation model should be universal and not refer only to one type of project. Universality should also be expressed in the opportunity of applying the model to different types of evaluation: initial, ongoing, and final.
4. Modeling should be carried out using the adopted integrated approach based on selected concepts and theories.

5. The principle of priority of learning processes over the static application of knowledge resources necessary for evaluation is adopted.
6. Thanks to the feedback and constant updating of the knowledge base, there should be dynamic adaptation to occurring changes and permanent improvement of project evaluation.
7. The learning processes of this evaluation model can be presented as a sequence of actions repeated iteratively. The steps that create each repeated sequence are analogous and can be isolated as a result of subsequent approximations and computational experiments.
8. The developed evaluation model should ensure easy implementation and the possibility of verification using empirical data.
9. The modeling process should be divided into two stages: general and more detailed and formalized, which may facilitate the implementation and empirical verification of the model.
10. The model should be implemented using AI technology, in particular Rule Based Systems and GAI.
11. The empirical basis for verifying the evaluation model may be experience in the field of knowledge discovery and multicriteria project sorting.

The results related to modeling the improvement of evaluation as an action system can be presented in two forms. The first is the general model concept created using an integrated methodological approach. This concept is a description of the system model with a lower degree of detail. The second form of results is a formalized mathematical model built on the basis of the concept of a general model. The use of AI methods inspired by mathematical theories facilitates the development of formalized models.

The developed model for project evaluation may be largely heuristic in nature, use knowledge-based rules, GAI, and, in some cases, be based on unmeasurable evaluation criteria and the discovery of knowledge in symbolic form as a result of the learning process. The use of mathematical tools helpful in building a formalized model of the action system may facilitate its implementation and further empirical research.

Applications of Rule-Based Systems

Researchers of the theory and practice of project management are looking for opportunities to construct models based to a greater extent on the analysis of qualitative data and expert knowledge. The importance of AI technologies that enable the discovery and generation of knowledge useful for project managers is constantly increasing. A significant frame of reference for conducting such considerations and research may be an integrated systems approach that takes into account not only the achievements of management sciences but also the recent progress made in computational intelligence and GAI methods. This approach creates conditions for improving the previously used project evaluation systems and introducing knowledge-based rules, enabling the implementation of universal methodological solutions of an interdisciplinary nature.

In project management, systems that use knowledge-based rules (RBS) for reason over data, automatic decision-making, and providing expert advice can potentially have many applications. The use of systems with a rule-based knowledge base, for example, for multicriteria classification (sorting) of projects, may improve the effectiveness, speed up and simplify the evaluation process, compared to evaluation based solely on the knowledge and intuition of experts due to the following reasons:

1. Knowledge stored in a knowledge base can be obtained from many experts. The project evaluation system may therefore be characterized by greater knowledge resources compared to selected, individual experts. However, this is not always the case so far because KBS uses domain knowledge to a limited extent, and when solving general problems, sometimes better results are provided by a human expert.
2. The use of KBS is often much cheaper compared to the labor costs of experts, who sometimes need to be engaged many times to perform repetitive tasks. In the case of automated knowledge discovery, large costs are incurred mainly during the design of the intelligent system and the implementation of the knowledge base. It is much less expensive to update this database later, and it is possible to use KBS multiple times.
3. The advice suggested by RBS may be available at any time in a constant manner, and the use of experts' knowledge depends on their availability and psychophysical condition.
4. KBS facilitate the provision of advice remotely (using an application available via a computer network) to a larger number of people than in the case of the need to provide personal contacts with experts.
5. The use of expert advice is time-limited, and in the case of KBS, it is possible to analyze various variants of solutions and search for optimal projects.
6. For typical situations, a system with a well-prepared knowledge base can classify projects faster compared to average experts.

After considering the above comments, the following desirable features of the evaluation system model can be formulated:

1. It enables the representation and collection of a clear form of knowledge resulting even from empirical data that are difficult to analyze, which can develop economic imagination, helping understanding and appropriate interpretation of the results of the evaluation process.
2. The discovery of knowledge that develops lateral thinking and the analysis of socioeconomic phenomena from various perspectives are ensured. Thanks to this development of creativity, the collected knowledge can be used not only

to conduct evaluations but also to define new ideas and interesting projects. The weaknesses of the assessed projects may result in the strengths of subsequent new project concepts. What constitutes previously diagnosed threats can be transformed into opportunities for subsequent projects.

3. It processes empirical data about projects, which are generally characterized by inconsistency and uncertainty. The evaluation process considers the specific feelings and attitudes of experts, and their perception of reality is subjective. Thanks to this, you can avoid searching for 'absolute and objective truth' that does not exist in practice. The development of the evaluation process should result from a compromise between objective evaluation criteria and the integrated attitudes of subjective experts.

4. It enables independent analysis of the results of evaluation carried out by experts, identification and rejection of the results of the evaluation process resulting from obvious errors made by these experts.

5. It comprehensively covers the evaluation process, constitutes a whole with dynamic properties, takes into account the nonlinearity of the decision-making process thanks to the feedback loop, and is characterized by nondeterministic functioning.

6. It is characterized by adaptability and responds to internal and external changes of the evaluation system.

7. It allows, on the one hand, to decompose (break down) the system into smaller elements (which are interconnected) and, on the other hand, to aggregate these elements into one system. It is possible to precisely and consistently (for the entire modeling process) distinguish the internal elements of the system from the elements belonging to the environment.

8. It is characterized by reliability – that is, correct implementation of activities related to the project evaluation process.

9. The evaluation is interdisciplinary and multi-aspect enabling multicriteria assessment using the principle of dominance.

10. It enables universal evaluation of many types of projects.

11. The basis for building the model is a systems approach.

12. It is characterized by applicability, that is, its relatively simple implementation and practical verification are possible.

13. Collection and analysis of empirical data, knowledge discovery, and decision support in real time are ensured.

14. Discovered knowledge is stored in a computer knowledge base in a human-readable form which allows for relatively easy presentation.

15. The system is designed to learn from past examples (evaluated projects).

16. It is resistant to contradictory evaluations and expert attitudes and copes with logically exclusive, extremely different values of evaluation criteria, the values of which may be characterized by discontinuity and lack of chronological consistency.

Adopting a systemic paradigm and relying on innovative AI technologies creates grounds for taking into account the multi-aspect and difficult-to-measure features of the projects, as well as resources collected in knowledge bases and relating to the hidden knowledge of experts participating in previous evaluation processes. The design and implementation of an evaluation model require an appropriate selection of the methodological approaches useful for multicriteria project analysis.

Methodological Approaches for Multicriteria Knowledge-Based Project Analysis

The advantages of rough set models justify their use as one of the most important elements in the integrated approach and AI-driven knowledge-based evaluation system (described in more detail in Chapter 4). These types of models make it possible to take into account the uncertainty of conclusions, which may result from doubts about the quality of knowledge describing a given reality – that is, its accuracy, completeness, and reliability. When conducting evaluations, there may also be difficulties in accurately and precisely describing complex and qualitative socioeconomic and environmental phenomena.

High requirements and challenges related to the evaluation of contemporary projects result from their diverse features, uniqueness, and non-repeatability. In evaluation processes, they are described using many different attributes. Models used during evaluation can only constitute a simplified description of the real world, which uses a selected and significantly limited number of attributes (criteria). These selected attributes allow the identification of parameters describing the evaluated projects and enable distinguishing some of them from others. Distinguishing involves finding similarities and differences between attributes, as well as positive and negative features of both.

Rough sets are one of the mathematically inspired approaches supporting the definition of rough and fuzzy concepts in multicriteria KBS. This approach is used in knowledge discovery processes, data mining, and solving many problems related to decision support. Its classic version is based on equivalence relations, according to which the attributes taken into account are nominal. This assumption is difficult to meet for many decision-making problems occurring in business practice. For this reason, work is being undertaken to generalize rough sets aimed at modifying the mathematical apparatus from the point of view of practical applications.

Multicriteria analysis using generalized rough set theory provides an opportunity to ensure appropriate accuracy in defining vague concepts in a knowledge-based project evaluation. According to rough set theory, these concepts can be described using lower and upper approximations (Pawlak, 1991). These approximations are built from elementary sets (elementary concepts, knowledge granules). The accuracy of defining vague concepts improves as the number of attributes describing individual objects increases.

Information about the examined objects described by the same specific set of attributes can be written in the form of an attribute-value table (information

Table 3.1 Attribute-value table

U\A	Conditional attribute a_1	Conditional attribute a_2	Conditional attribute a_3	. . .	Conditional attribute a_m
Object x_1	$f(x_1, a_1)$	$f(x_1, a_2)$	$f(x_1, a_3)$	. . .	$f(x_1, a_m)$
Object x_2	$f(x_2, a_1)$	$f(x_2, a_2)$	$f(x_2, a_3)$	. . .	$f(x_2, a_m)$
Object x_3	$f(x_3, a_1)$	$f(x_3, a_2)$	$f(x_3, a_3)$	. . .	$f(x_3, a_m)$
. . .	. . .	. . .	. . .	. . .	. . .
Object x_n	$f(x_n, a_1)$	$f(x_n, a_2)$	$f(x_n, a_3)$	. . .	$f(x_n, a_m)$

Source: Inspired by (Pawlak, 1991)

table). Table 3.1 shows the use of an information table model consisting of objects (evaluated projects) $x_1, x_2, x_3, \ldots, x_n$ and attributes ($a_1, a_2, a_3, \ldots, a_m$). The symbols appearing in the upper left corner of the table mean: U (the universe) is a finite set of objects (projects), and A is the given set of attributes (criteria).

For individual objects appearing in the rows of this table, the values of the information function reflecting the connections between individual objects and the attribute values describing them are entered. It is possible to enter in these lines the number of points awarded to various projects in the evaluation process. Information about the evaluated projects, which is stored using individual attributes (evaluation criteria), creates the knowledge system.

The foundation on which this classic rough sets approach is based is the indiscernibility relation (Pawlak, 1991). This approach is called the classical rough set approach (CRSA), or sometimes also Pawlak Sets or Indiscernibility-Based Rough Sets, to distinguish it from generalized rough sets developed as part of many research streams. The most important features of CRSA that cause great interest among representatives of theory and practice include the following properties:

1. The simple interpretation of the mathematical description makes it relatively easy to understand, even for people with limited knowledge of mathematics. Algorithms based on rough sets usually function relatively quickly and are not very complex. These algorithms are characterized by tolerance for inconsistencies and missing information in the input datasets.
2. The basis for data analysis is indiscernibility relations, and indiscernible elements create knowledge granules in the form of elementary sets that can be used to distinguish crisp sets (i.e., conventional sets) from rough sets – they cannot be presented as the sum of any elementary sets.
3. Ease of generalization and extension of CRSA capabilities is achieved for better practice applicability. For example, the rough sets generalization (based on the dominance principle) is particularly helpful when solving multicriteria problems.
4. The possibility of applying this theory to data analysis aimed at discovering knowledge – hidden relationships in datasets usually stored in decision tables. These tables are a preliminary (simply modifiable) form of

representing hidden knowledge regarding, for example, the experiences of practitioners and experts. Such experiences can be written in the form of decision rules reflecting the relationships between conditional attributes and the decision attribute (determining the classification of objects). These analyses often result in decision rules that would be difficult to identify intuitively without the use of rough sets.

5. Ease of processing information and knowledge obtained empirically (quantitative and qualitative). A clear form of results in the form of decision rules simplifying the interpretation of the results obtained. These rules create a record of expert knowledge in the form of a rule-based knowledge base useful in building KBS and supporting project evaluation.

6. Rough sets are suitable in the process of analyzing poorly structured and blurred data, which often occur in socioeconomic analyses. They cannot be properly characterized using classical set theory. Rough sets, though, are not an alternative to classical set theory, and they do not replace it. However, they extend the possibilities of mathematical tools (based on the concept of a set) to include the analysis of vague concepts, which can be represented using two crisp concepts.

7. Possibility of reducing redundant information and knowledge and building a smaller (than the original) set of attributes sufficient to properly describe the analyzed objects. Minimization also applies to the number of generated decision rules obtained based on the analysis of attributes stored in decision tables.

As previously mentioned, for the purposes of solving practical problems, it is worth accepting some minor differences between objects and partial departures from full compliance of the indiscernibility relation with the equivalence relation (regarding reflexivity, symmetry, and transitivity). Therefore, many approaches have been developed to generalize the capabilities of CRSA, such as the following.

1. Replacing the indiscernibility relation with a similarity relation, which is reflexive, but in this approach it is not transitive and not symmetric (Slowinski & Vanderpooten, 2000); this enables applications in multicriteria decision support systems analogous to outranking relations (Figueira et al., 2016).

2. Based on tolerance relation – in this approach, reflexive and symmetrical, but not transitive – with a similarity test based on the value of the so-called similarity threshold, which can be used in various types of multicriteria classification systems (tolerant rough set classifier) (Yun & Ma, 2006).

3. The use of the Pareto dominance relation, which, compared to the indiscernibility relation, is reflexive and transitive, but not symmetrical.

It was assumed that the third methodological approach mentioned above, which is derived from CRSA, is the most useful when evaluating projects.

This approach is consistent with the Pareto approach, and using it, a relatively objective multicriteria sorting process can be carried out, in which projects described by the values of the evaluation criteria are compared. DRSA is used to solve typical multicriteria decision-making problems – that is, ranking, selection, sorting, and others.

The use of the dominance relations concept enables the introduction of decision rules taking into account the approximation of preference relations to solve decision-making problems related to multicriteria selection and ranking of evaluated projects. According to the DRSA the approximate preference relation can be based on the gradient dominance relation (Greco et al., 2002). The practical interpretation of this principle (semantic correlation) for the two evaluated projects is as follows: If the first project, for all evaluation criteria, was evaluated at least as good as the second one the first project should have a decision attribute at least as good as the second one.

The undoubted advantage of DRSA is its practical usefulness in project evaluation – examples (projects) for learning evaluation systems can be entered into individual rows of the decision table. This is a way of recording objects known from CRSA. According to the DRSA the attributes (evaluation criteria) describing the evaluated objects are ordered according to preferences. It is possible to use the integration of set approximations with the dominance relation. CRSA should be replaced with DRSA when at least one of the conditional attributes has criterion properties (i.e., has a preferentially ordered domain) and there are specific and preferentially ordered decision classes to which decisions related to individual objects are assigned.

As in the case of CRSA, the DRSA divides attributes into conditional (for DRSA these are criteria) and decision ones, most often stored in a decision table – the attribute-value table is supplemented with a column with the decision attribute values. There should be a semantic correlation between the attributes stored in the table in accordance with the principle of dominance. Thanks to this, the decision rules generated on the basis of the decision table reflect the dependencies and connections between the conditional attributes (criteria) and decision ones, taking into account the principle of dominance.

To summarize, among the more important features of DRSA, which exceed those of CRSA in solving multicriteria decision support problems, are the following (Błaszczyński et al., 2022):

1. Implementation of learning and knowledge discovery focused on multiple criteria decision aiding.
2. Taking into account the preferential order of conditional criteria.
3. The ability to collect simple and easy-to-obtain information about preferences from decision-makers and generate recommendations that are clear and can be easily justified.

4. Semantic correlation between conditional criteria and the decision attribute consistent with the principle of dominance.
5. Discretization procedures for quantitative attributes are not required, as is the case with many CRSA-compliant algorithms.
6. A clearer form of knowledge represented using rules based on the dominance relation, due to their more extensive syntax, which results from replacing considerations of the indiscernibility of objects with the study of a larger number of relations – equality and outranking relations (up and down).
7. Decision rules generated using algorithms based on the DRSA constitute a preference model discovered from empirical data.

The newer DRSA, on the one hand, is characterized by the advantages of the classic CRSA – that is, it enables data analysis (in conditions of risk and uncertainty) related to solving problems: classification (sorting into previously defined decision classes), ordering (ranking of variants), and selection of objects. On the other hand, it is a practically useful approach valuable in the process of supporting multicriteria decisions – for example, project evaluation. The evaluation process of these types of projects is based on many preferentially ordered criteria. DRSA-compliant analysis of data (preliminarily recorded in the decision table) leads to the generation of decision rules that take into account the preferential relationships occurring in this data. They may be useful in the process of classifying new projects, that is, those not used in the process of generating decision rules (i.e. learning the evaluation system).

References

Ahmadi Eftekhari, N., Mani, S., Bakhshi, I., & Mani, S. (2022). Project manager competencies for dealing with socio-technical complexity: A grounded theory construction. *Systems, 10*(5), 161. https://doi.org/10.3390/systems10050161

Alvarenga, J. C., Branco, R. R., Guedes, A. L. A., Soares, C. A. P., & Silva, W. D. S. E. (2019). The project manager core competencies to project success. *International Journal of Managing Projects in Business, 13*(2), 277–292. https://doi.org/10.1108/IJMPB-12-2018-0274

Azevedo De Souza, L., Gomes Costa, H., & Oliveira De Araujo, F. (2022). Prioritizing criteria to evaluate project success: Modeling with the Analytic Hierarchy Process (AHP): Empirical study in a Brazilian health organization. *International Journal of the Analytic Hierarchy Process, 14*(1). https://doi.org/10.13033/ijahp.v14i1.913

Barcaui, A., & Monat, A. (2023). Who is better in project planning? Generative artificial intelligence or project managers? *Project Leadership and Society, 4*, 100101. https://doi.org/10.1016/j.plas.2023.100101

Błaszczyński, J., Greco, S., Matarazzo, B., & Szeląg, M. (2022). Dominance-based rough set approach: Basic ideas and main trends. In S. Greco, V.

Mousseau, J. Stefanowski, & C. Zopounidis (Eds.), *Intelligent decision support systems* (pp. 353–382). Springer International Publishing. https://doi.org/10.1007/978-3-030-96318-7_18

Figueira, J. R., Mousseau, V., & Roy, B. (2016). ELECTRE methods. In S. Greco, M. Ehrgott, & J. R. Figueira (Eds.), *Multiple criteria decision analysis* (Vol. 233, pp. 155–185). Springer New York. https://doi.org/10.1007/978-1-4939-3094-4_5

Greco, S., Matarazzo, B., & Slowinski, R. (2002). Rough sets methodology for sorting problems in presence of multiple attributes and criteria. *European Journal of Operational Research, 138*(2), 247–259. https://doi.org/10.1016/S0377-2217(01)00244-2

Grzeszczyk, T. A. (2018). *Mixed intelligent systems.* Palgrave – Springer International Publishing. https://doi.org/10.1007/978-3-319-91158-8

Hashfi, M. I., & Raharjo, T. (2023). Exploring the challenges and impacts of artificial intelligence implementation in project management: A systematic literature review. *International Journal of Advanced Computer Science and Applications, 14*(9). https://doi.org/10.14569/IJACSA.2023.0140940

Marhraoui, M. A. (2023). Digital skills for project managers: A systematic literature review. *Procedia Computer Science, 219*, 1591–1598. https://doi.org/10.1016/j.procs.2023.01.451

Odeh, M. (2023). The role of artificial intelligence in project management. *IEEE Engineering Management Review, 51*(4), 20–22. https://doi.org/10.1109/EMR.2023.3309756

Oscar, L. H., Cerqueira, L. C., Cunha, P. H., & Qualharini, E. L. (2023). Generative design in civil construction: A case study in Brazil. *Frontiers in Built Environment, 9*, 1150767. https://doi.org/10.3389/fbuil.2023.1150767

Pawlak, Z. (1991). *Rough sets: Theoretical aspects of reasoning about data* (1991st ed.). Kluwer Academic Publishers.

Salleh, M. H., & Aziz, K. Ab. (2022). Artificial intelligence augmented project management. In A. Asmawi (Ed.), *Proceedings of the international conference on technology and innovation management (ICTIM 2022)* (Vol. 228, pp. 274–284). Atlantis Press International BV. https://doi.org/10.2991/978-94-6463-080-0_24

Samset, K., & Volden, G. H. (2022). Closing the loop. In T. M. Williams, K. Samset, & G. H. Volden (Eds.), *The front-end of large public projects* (1st ed., pp. 158–190). Routledge. https://doi.org/10.4324/9781003257172-7

Slowinski, R., & Vanderpooten, D. (2000). A generalized definition of rough approximations based on similarity. *IEEE Transactions on Knowledge and Data Engineering, 12*(2), 331–336. https://doi.org/10.1109/69.842271

Taboada, I., Daneshpajouh, A., Toledo, N., & De Vass, T. (2023). Artificial intelligence enabled project management: A systematic literature review. *Applied Sciences, 13*(8), 5014. https://doi.org/10.3390/app13085014

Thamhain, H. J. (2013). Contemporary methods for evaluating complex project proposals. *Journal of Industrial Engineering International, 9*(1), 34. https://doi.org/10.1186/2251-712X-9-34

Vanhoucke, M. (2023a). Project data. In M. Vanhoucke (Ed.), *The illusion of control* (pp. 181–187). Springer Nature Switzerland. https://doi.org/10.1007/978-3-031-31785-9_10

Vanhoucke, M. (2023b). The data-driven project manager. In M. Vanhoucke (Eds.), *The illusion of control* (pp. 29–48). Springer Nature Switzerland. https://doi.org/10.1007/978-3-031-31785-9_3

Yun, O., & Ma, J. (2006). Land cover classification based on tolerant rough set. *International Journal of Remote Sensing, 27*(14), 3041–3047. https://doi.org/10.1080/01431160600702368

4 AI-Driven Knowledge-Based Evaluation

Preliminary Comments about Evaluation System Modeling

Evaluation processes play an increasingly important role in the management of various types of organizations, especially in connection with the need to minimize the risk of unique and complex activities. Evaluators should take into account achievements resulting from the development of various scientific fields and disciplines. The achievements accumulated in the social sciences are of the greatest importance, but progress in various areas related to computer science and data science should also be noted. Evaluation processes should therefore be viewed from the perspectives of different scientific disciplines and using a transdisciplinary approach. This means the possibility of using evaluation methods, techniques and tools from a variety of scientific disciplines.

Evaluation is sometimes even perceived as a new, independent scientific discipline that is used to describe the surrounding reality, and contributes to understanding the impact of human actions on this reality. Systematic research into these issues is carried out both in scientific research and in evaluation (Patton, 2018). The implementation of systematic evaluation research should contribute to improving social conditions in particular political and organizational environments (Rossi et al., 2019).

Evaluation most often involves estimating the value of, for example, policies, portfolios, programs, projects, selected products, and entire organizations. According to the classic and very well-known definition, evaluation of a selected object is a systematic process of examining its quality, merit, and value (worth) (Scriven, 1991). Generally, the definitions emphasize the need to systematically collect and analyze data and information regarding activities and outcomes of projects and programs aimed at making their judgments, which may be useful in improving them, further developing their effectiveness and/or increasing understanding (Patton & Campbell-Patton, 2021). Evaluation carried out in project management means collecting data and analyzing it to measure progress aimed at achieving the assumed goal.

DOI: 10.4324/9781003341611-4

The growing importance of evaluation in business and project management is reflected in the creation of increasingly better theoretical achievements and more and more significant and useful practical recommendations. This increase in interest in evaluation is understandable from the point of view of the growing need to improve the quality of project activities and entire organizations. Appropriate implementation of evaluation studies can prevent errors in project planning and implementation, as well as provide a reliable and objective justification for decisions made regarding the allocation of increasingly difficult-to-access resources. Efficient evaluation and monitoring enable systematic adaptation to constant changes in the environment of the organization and the projects it implements. Effective monitoring and evaluation should support learning processes, involve key stakeholders, and meet decision needs (Amin et al., 2023).

Correct implementation of project evaluation is helpful in diagnosing areas requiring improvement not only within individual projects but in entire organizations, and as a result, it promotes continuous improvement of these organizations. Improvement is achieved by making the necessary adjustments and increasing the effectiveness of the projects. Evaluation supporting continuous improvement of the organization contributes to boosting the effectiveness of management, control, learning, and knowledge management in organizations. Learning and knowledge management should concern not only successful projects but also unsuccessful ones, which means learning from successes and mistakes (Samset & Volden, 2022).

Evaluation of successful and unsuccessful projects is a unique, complex, and often challenging process. The literature review shows that only accepting the multi-aspect nature of evaluation carried out taking into account many dimensions creates the basis for a meaningful conception of multidimensional project evaluation (Rode et al., 2022). Therefore, as part of project evaluation studies, the obtained multi-aspect effects should be predicted or measured. Modern project evaluation systems cannot be limited only to quantitative economic and financial factors. These systems should also take into account various aspects of broad strategic importance, difficult-to-measure sustainable development of organizations, regions, and entire countries. Evaluation research should be comprehensive and interdisciplinary in nature and cover many aspects, such as environmental, social, economic, technological, scientific and research, organizational, cultural, political, and legal.

Due to the multi-aspect nature of evaluation, the criteria used for different projects may differ significantly. These criteria may be related primarily to efficiency, effectiveness, sustainability, usefulness, accuracy, relevance, and long-term outcomes – the strategic impact of actions in the area of project implementation. Among the criteria mentioned, efficiency is of primary importance, as it correlates moderately strongly to overall project success (Serrador & Turner, 2015). In addition to efficiency and the previously mentioned criteria, project evaluation may take into account a certain number of other types of specific criteria selected for the stakeholders involved, project context, and organizational goals – for example, stakeholder satisfaction, future potential of the organization, and customer benefits (He et al., 2022). When taking into account a very diverse set of criteria, problems may arise due to their usually difficult-to-measure and qualitative nature and problems in presenting their value in quantitative and monetary form.

In publications on evaluation, relatively little space is devoted to the use of systems based on new ICT and AI technologies. There is too little information about the possibilities resulting from the use of these technologies, despite the dynamic increase in interest in AI issues in recent years and the possibilities of supporting the evaluation of various complex, dynamically changing projects located in an environment characterized by significant uncertainty. There are known examples in the literature of the use of AI to support the implementation of the teaching process, assess student projects, and take into account both the technical and creative components when issuing grades (Divasón et al., 2023). Interesting research concerns the possibility of using a data-driven research framework based on ML for the analytics of construction projects (Uddin et al., 2022). The area of using AI methods in evaluation is still little explored, and the literature draws attention to the need for further work on possible criteria domains for AI application in evaluation (Montrosse-Moorhead, 2023). Certainly, in the near future, AI will enrich evaluators and project management professions in various project management knowledge areas (Fridgeirsson et al., 2021).

This chapter draws attention to the possibilities resulting from a knowledge-based evaluation carried out with the support of the integrated approach, RBS, and GAI. Combining different approaches and concepts makes it possible to consider the quantitative and qualitative aspects in project evaluation. The proposed solution fundamentally differs from the classic approaches to business project evaluation, primarily concerned with financial and economic analyses. The primary methods of financial evaluation of projects are based on simple measures that do not take into account changes in the value of money over time (e.g., a simple rate of return) or more complex discount indicators that take these changes into account, for example, the net present value (NPV) and the Internal Rate of Return.

Classic methods and indicators are well known and characterized in many publications in the field of finance. If it is necessary to carry out multi-aspect evaluation of projects, it is not appropriate to conduct only financial analyses and use only quantitative financial indicators, mathematical methods, or quantitative multicriteria methods. The financial result cannot be the only or main evaluation criterion. The evaluated projects may be characterized by high NPV values, but at the same time, they do not provide the expected value to various groups of stakeholders. Analyses should be integrated regarding the simultaneous optimization of the values of various indicators, for example, maximizing NPV and project value (Szwarcfiter et al., 2023).

It is increasingly necessary to estimate benefits measured in broader social and environmental perspectives. It is also important to measure and evaluate the long-term positive effects of projects on their socioeconomic environment. Therefore, it is practically useful to use not only monetary indicators, but also qualitative nonmonetary methods and universal multicriteria evaluation methods.

The use of universal multicriteria evaluation methods sometimes entails the consequences of a lack of objectivity when conducting evaluation. The use of multicriteria evaluation measures seemingly leads to greater objectivity compared, for example, to systems based on one or two selected criteria. Meanwhile, during evaluation, not only objective aspects but also subjective aspects of evaluation should be taken into account. A review of the literature on project evaluation shows that even multicriteria evaluations are focused mainly on objective aspects and do not take into account subjective aspects that concern the complex, uncertain, temporal, dynamic, and subjective nature of many evaluated projects (Haass & Guzman, 2020).

In practice, multicriteria analyses are mainly used by experts who often take on significant challenges related to the need to consider the complexity, uncertainty, dynamics, and subjective nature of the evaluated projects. This means the need to rely on the knowledge, experience, and subjective value systems of expert panel participants. Expert evaluation methods have a number of imperfections because evaluators often come from various backgrounds and have different experiences and attitudes. There may also often be suspicions of bias and a lack of objectivity among experts. Additionally, it is not easy to assemble a group of experts with appropriate qualifications and availability. Expert knowledge is tacit, and therefore it is sometimes difficult to find objective justification for the decisions of specialists engaged in assessment and to intuitively identify clear rules reflecting their reasoning and justification for the decisions made. There are also often problems with the availability of knowledge from previous evaluation processes. This knowledge is usually not used, and its management is very difficult.

An important justification for promoting AI-driven knowledge-based evaluation is that the issue of evaluation is a poorly structured decision-making problem in conditions of high uncertainty. This uncertainty results from many external and internal factors. External factors include the variability and turbulent nature of the socioeconomic and political environment of the evaluated projects. The guidelines resulting from various strategic analyses of the environment are often relatively unclear, subjective, ambiguous, subject to frequent changes, and have limited usefulness for many projects. External and internal factors are described not only using quantitative measures, but most often imperatively also considering nonmeasurable qualitative criteria.

An additional source of uncertainty may be the resources of knowledge possessed by the experts carrying out evaluations, whose decisions may result from various unmeasurable factors, such as beliefs, attitudes towards the existing reality, personal, psychological, social, or cultural conditions. Another justification for the development and use of AI-driven knowledge-based evaluation is the growing requirement for evaluation, which results from the still-open discussion on understanding project success. An inspiration for conducting this type of research is, for example, the Phoenix phenomenon – that is, the evaluation of innovative projects that, paradoxically, can be both a failure and a success (Midler & Alochet, 2023).

The genesis of undertaking research on AI-driven knowledge-based evaluation results from the recognition of the need and possibility of conducting interdisciplinary methodological research on improving multi-aspect project evaluation. The main goal of the research undertaken is to enable comprehensive evaluation of projects using an integrated approach and knowledge discovery through learning. The goal formulated in this way opens an extensive research space, the specification of which is possible as a result of the application of concepts and theories influencing contemporary management and solutions resulting from the development of AI technologies, in particular GAI and KBS.

It was assumed that there is a need and possibility of objectifying, simplifying, and accelerating the project evaluation process by using computer-aided analysis and classification of knowledge and taking into account in the current project evaluation, empirical knowledge from experts who worked in previous evaluation processes. Additionally, it was presumed that it is useful to apply AI methods and adaptive evaluation measures in the form of decision rules.

The proposed knowledge-based evaluation system enables the generation of decision rules using a separate set of projects belonging to the learning set. The project evaluation verification process can be performed based on projects saved in the test set. The division into learning and testing subsets is typical for AI methods, in which the process of learning and improving the functioning of an intelligent system is carried out by acquiring new knowledge useful in solving the desired problem. This knowledge is discovered based on empirical data related to past evaluation processes. Such empirical knowledge is usually a good generalization of the experiences of experts who classify projects. The proposed intelligent system based on empirical knowledge enables the management of such knowledge and its use in the evaluation processes of subsequent projects (which were not previously used to learn the evaluation system).

An additional advantage of the proposed solution is the ability to improve the knowledge-based evaluation system by iteratively modifying the set of training projects and the rule-based knowledge base. The main manifestation of improvement is the increase in the accuracy of project classification by the intelligent system. Another advantage is the relatively easy way of building trust in the AI methods used thanks to a human-readable computer representation of expert knowledge, which allows for easy justification of decisions made regarding the assignment of evaluated projects to previously adopted decision classes. A human-readable representation of knowledge results from the use of methods of recording knowledge in the form of generated decision rules.

The necessity to carry out this type of research results from the needs of project evaluators, who may find this type of methodological support valuable. The usefulness is confirmed when a general concept of the evaluation system model is proposed, its improvement and practical verification of the model that is associated with its implementation and research conducted using a set of empirical data on the evaluation of projects in the past. This data may concern the results of multicriteria evaluation carried out by experts in accordance with the adopted quantitative and qualitative criteria. The use of these evaluation criteria should lead to a specific assignment of the evaluated projects, for example, to three decision classes – that is, projects completely rejected, positively evaluated but not qualified for financing, and accepted for implementation. Projects from individual decision classes can be divided into subsets: learning and testing. Using projects from the learning set, it is possible to generate decision rules and build a rule knowledge base. In turn, the application of this knowledge base enables the evaluation process of projects from the test set.

The integrated approach, computer experiments based on decision tables, generation of decision rules, and logical inference using the DRSA mentioned in Chapter 3 proved useful in the research process. The subsequent sections in this chapter result from the presented research goal and the adopted assumptions about the need and possibilities of AI-driven knowledge-based evaluation using an integrated approach and knowledge discovery through learning.

Integrated Approach

The considerations in this section concern the possibility of using classic concepts and theories as well as newer ones that influence contemporary management as a basis for choosing solutions supported by AI methods, in particular GAI and DRSA (which is the selected multicriteria approach). Recent achievements and development of GAI are an incentive to conduct research on the possibility of combined use of GAI and the abovementioned approach related to RBS. The integrated use of both AI technologies can ensure, on the one hand, the generation of useful decision rules and, on the other hand, generative support for dynamic improvement and expansion of rule knowledge bases.

The integration of GAI and DRSA can effectively support the automation of the processes of building, updating, and using the evaluation model by ensuring the generation of subsequent decision rules with less involvement of experts. It is necessary to remember that the participation of evaluators when creating knowledge bases is essential. Automation resulting from the use of AI technology plays an important but only supporting role. It is mandatory to take care not only of technological aspects but also those related to the human factor and take into account inspirations related to theories that have a significant impact on contemporary project and organizational management.

Contemporary management is influenced by theories that question normative theory and offer the use of alternative perspectives in decision-making processes. Existing theories shape the understanding of how management research and practice are conducted in different ways. For example, the normative (rational-analytical) theory and the behavioral (intuitive-emotional) approach are largely mutually exclusive. It is difficult to assume that managers always make fully rational decisions within formalized and structured processes. In such a case, simple and deterministic methods of supporting rational-analytical analyses would be sufficient. Assuming the rationality of decisions made renders it impossible to take into account subjective- and personality-related human factors, which often have a strong impact on decision-making processes. The behavioral approach is worth considering, especially in cases of evaluating projects related to social and environmental aspects – for example, socially responsible investment (Gamel et al., 2022).

It is therefore reasonable to seek an integrated model for decision-making under uncertainty that can simultaneously incorporate normative and behavioral approaches. AI technologies can be helpful in building such a model in which information, being an intermediary in multistage and multi-stakeholder decision processes, allows taking into account uncertainty and behavioral aspects (Chai et al., 2021).

In striving to improve project evaluation, it is therefore desirable to abandon isolationism (using only a selected theory and approach) and apply an integrated (interdisciplinary) methodological approach supported by selected systems approaches, the methodology of management sciences and consistent with several theories related to information and knowledge management. This approach should enable the management of knowledge useful during evaluation and take into account the uncertainty of the evaluation process and the often immeasurable nature of evaluation criteria. It is also necessary to consider the nonlinearity of the system when using a learning system with a feedback loop. Thanks to this, as the environment changes, the evaluation system can be improved by evolving the principles of its operation.

The methodology of management sciences includes a significant number of developed and interpenetrating management concepts. Particularly useful are concepts that enable carrying out multidimensional analyses in turbulent environments and the presence of significant uncertainty resulting from the dynamics and complexity of modern socioeconomic systems. It is therefore useful to implement a systems approach and methodological pluralism – that is, the application of various approaches, methods, concepts, and techniques. This solution makes it possible to take into account the complexity, multi-aspect nature, and variability of the described reality regarding the evaluated projects.

The integrated approach can therefore be based on inspirations from selected theories known from management sciences – that is, the systems approach, situational approach, behavioral theory (taking into account the human factor), theory of organizational learning, and knowledge management. The application of learning and knowledge management processes enables continuous improvements thanks to the implementation of the principles of a learning (intelligent) organization. Additionally, it may be useful to assume the need to take into account the behavioral approach supporting analytical computer analyses of decision-making problems.

The generalized rough set theory based on modifications of classical set theory may be helpful in considering the behavioral trend during computer analyses. Set theory has been used many times in management sciences – for example, in the process of modeling organizations. As mentioned earlier in this chapter, the generalized theory can form the basis of the proposed learning system based on empirical examples related to project evaluation. The application of the abovementioned theories creates conditions for an integrated approach in the processes of modeling evaluation systems, taking into account systemic knowledge management, soft issues related to evaluators, and continuous improvement adapted to the current situation.

Figure 4.1 shows that the use of an integrated approach enables the synthesis of various complementary trends and management concepts. Finding a single-minded quest for management theory is unattainable, and it is desirable to supplement the applied theories with behavioral factors, such as morality, creativity, imagination, choice, responsibility, and purpose (Joullié & Gould, 2023). Applying only one selected normative perspective when conducting research in management sciences is not very reasonable. If the assumption is made to reject the use of only this perspective, it is possible to positively look at, for example, groupthink (group decision-making) as a plausible alternative to other managerial decision-making theories (Deal et al., 2023).

Groupthink and other extensive decision-making approaches involve the use of complex information and decision-making structures and the integration of information from many heterogeneous sources and the generalization of the acquired knowledge. When using this type of model, it is worth implementing IT computing systems to better understand the high complexity of the problems of integrating information exchanged between many multiple interconnected actors occurring in diverse structures of mutual influence and sequential interactions (Klapper et al., 2021). Therefore, integrative concepts appear intuitively in the case of many currently recognized management concepts.

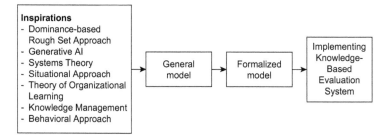

Figure 4.1 Integrated methodological approach in building the model of knowledge-based evaluation system

Classic management science literature states that systems and situational approaches enable the integration of classical and behavioral approaches and perspectives resulting from the use of quantitative theory based on mathematical models. It is not reasonable to limit oneself to only one approach known from management sciences. However, it is advisable to use selected integrating perspectives and rely on many mutually complementary concepts, tools, and techniques. (Griffin, 2021).

The systems approach has been known for a long time and is often used in management sciences. This type of approach makes it possible to obtain a holistic view of evaluation as a whole set of elements connected by relationships and functioning for a specific purpose. Typically, a distinction is made between the environment that shapes the system, its input, output, and feedback. General systems theory is useful in creating new integrated concepts and techniques that, on the one hand, draw inspiration from various fields and, on the other hand, are consistent with the basic functions of management. This theory is also useful in the field of project management and evaluation. Therefore, the terms 'project management' and those directly resulting from the systems view of reality are sometimes used interchangeably: 'systems management' or 'matrix management' (Kerzner, 2022).

The use of systems theory facilitates the understanding of complex phenomena, the analysis of complex processes, and serves to improve the functioning of the organization in a turbulent environment. This theory may be useful, for example, in developing integrated holistic frameworks for better understanding and improving metasystems for complex system governance performance (Rutherford, 2022). The use of holistic methodological approaches based on integration using a systems approach makes it easier to overcome the limitations resulting from focusing only on specific methods and tools (Sales, 2019).

The analysis of system evaluation should be accompanied by the previously mentioned situational approach, which makes it possible to consider the impact of factors describing the changing situation and determine the correct course of action in the system improvement process. The simultaneous use of universal approaches, such as behavioral approaches or those based on quantitative mathematical models, allows the identification of a method that is particularly useful in many different circumstances.

In turn, in accordance with the situational approach, there is an assumption that it is impossible to find one solution effective in many business situations. These situations are usually of a different, relative, and specific nature. It is therefore not possible to formulate general and universal organizational and management principles. This is due to the unique nature of individual organizations and their operating systems. Decision-making processes are adapted to specific and unique situations, which are largely shaped by the impact of a turbulent environment.

There is therefore justification for the combined use of systems and situational approaches during evaluation because it is then possible to consider, in particular, the uniqueness of the evaluated projects. It is easy to understand that the combined use of both approaches gives a better effect than, for example, only the systems approach. The situational approach compensates for some of the weaknesses of systems analysis resulting from its too general nature and relatively low usefulness in conditions of significant uncertainty. It is also its natural continuation and allows for specification in the often very diverse situations in which the organization operates.

Another inspiration for the integrated approach is the theory of organizational learning and knowledge management. There is extensive and well-known research on the problems and advantages resulting from the beneficial aspects of using knowledge management in organizations, which primarily concerns the management of knowledge content (Santhose & Lawrence, 2023). Management of such content focuses on improving several processes related to knowledge – that is, creating, storing, organizing, sharing, and using by various groups of organizational stakeholders (Lee, 2022). The concept of organizational learning is related to this, but has a more general character and covers many aspects of data, information, and knowledge (Fernandes & Machado, 2021). Many studies available in the literature indicate multi-level outcomes achieved through the implementation of learning organizational principles (Budhiraja et al., 2023). Organizational learning and knowledge management systems issues should be considered together in the context of created innovation and improved organizational performance (Luxmi, 2014).

Complex and multifaceted project evaluation processes should be supported by technologically advanced knowledge systems. Appropriately advanced systems can be built thanks to the development of AI, which creates favorable conditions for proposing agile and intelligent solutions. Thanks to the acquisition of knowledge in the system learning processes, it is possible to implement continuous and comprehensive improvement in conditions of uncertainty and turbulent system environment.

The next abovementioned behavioral approach emphasizes the fundamental importance of the human factor in organizations. In the project evaluation process, they refer to project stakeholders, and in particular to the evaluators. The need to take into account qualitative phenomena related to the human aspects of the evaluation process creates the premises for applying a systems approach in the process of building a learning system model. Systems of this type enable continuous improvement of project evaluation as a result of the use of methodological concepts based on symbolic computational intelligence and the implementation of soft computer algorithms. A systems approach integrated with AI tools allows for the inclusion of both quantitative and qualitative issues (e.g., social or environmental) in IT systems.

The synthesis of many management trends and concepts is therefore facilitated by the use of a systems approach in the process of building a general model of the evaluation system and a selected generalization of the rough set theory, enabling the formalization of considerations regarding multicriteria project analysis. This generalization is suitable in the process of modeling a learning system with a symbolic representation of knowledge for the purposes of implementing the improvement process. Generalization also facilitates the development of a model for acquiring knowledge as a result of learning and using it in the process of project evaluation. In this field, it is necessary to implement selected solutions related to information and knowledge management as well as solutions based on AI technologies analyzed on the basis of systems research.

The methodological concept based on DRSA enables the development of a relatively simple and useful evaluation model because computational intelligence methods can be introduced even when the essence of the project evaluation problem is not clearly and precisely defined. An additional justification is that the evaluation process is based primarily on empirical data and imprecise (intuitive) expert opinions. As a result of formalized modeling using the integrated approach and solutions resulting from DRSA, positive features of the model can be obtained.

The features used include multi-aspect nature resulting from the need and possibility of including in the evaluation model many socioeconomic and other aspects relating to both the features of the assessed projects and their environment. The built evaluation model may also be characterized by universality (the ability to evaluate various projects), as well as the possibility of dynamic adaptation to changes in the environment and permanent improvement of project evaluation achieved thanks to the possibility of constantly updating the rule knowledge base in the KBS.

Based on the integrated approach, it is useful for experts evaluating projects in terms of the measurability of quantitative and qualitative data, as well as the identification, processing, and measurement of expert knowledge saved and updated in the knowledge base. Ease of interpretation of the results is also ensured, because the knowledge is recorded in the form of decision rules that are easy to interpret and justify (also by humans), constituting a set of conditional attributes and a decision attribute.

The proposed approach also allows the implementation of an evaluation system that ensures comparability of evaluation results of different projects thanks to the fact that the evaluation is repeatable and it is possible to obtain similar results for similar projects. A different situation may arise in the case of subjective evaluations made by experts, who may be wrong. Evaluation supported by an integrated approach can also provide greater objectivity in the case of qualitative criteria because it reflects the knowledge and record of experience of a large group of experts, which can be recorded in a knowledge base.

DRSA applied as part of the integrated approach provides the possibility of multicriteria sorting of projects using the dominance relationship, ensuring the correct classification of projects into the appropriate decision classes in accordance with the adopted hierarchy of evaluation criteria. The ability to eliminate redundant information and knowledge is also important because

DRSA provides many mechanisms for reducing unnecessary attributes. There are also mechanisms available to easily check conflicting information and detect incorrect decisions regarding project evaluation.

Knowledge Discovery Through Learning

Knowledge management is one of the inspirations contributing to the formulation of the concepts of integrated approach and knowledge-based evaluation. Knowledge management includes several processes, primarily: acquiring and creating knowledge resources, storing them, transmitting and sharing them between employees in the organization, as well as using existing knowledge resources to obtain and consolidate a competitive advantage on the market. One of the ways to acquire knowledge (in technological terms) is to use algorithms for learning AI systems. The issues of knowledge discovery through learning include, among others, the following issues: AI technologies and systems as well as knowledge representation and reasoning. This area of knowledge is related to the study of AI systems in terms of the appropriate selection of knowledge representation and the creation of rules for managing this knowledge using reasoning computer programs. These programs allow computers to reason automatically in accordance with the algorithms used.

KBS have the ability to learn, adapt, and self-improve thanks to the acquired knowledge resulting from empirical data constituting learning examples. They may come, for example, from experts who use them to describe a specific reality and their subjective attitude towards it. Thanks to this, it is possible to discover knowledge not available by other methods. This knowledge can be stored in knowledge bases, which are the basic element of KBS. It is written using a specific knowledge representation method. This representation is analyzed from the point of view of two aspects of the system: internal and external. The internal one concerns the ability to store and modify knowledge. The external aspect is related to its possibilities of practical applications in solving desired problems, as well as its readability and comprehensibility, allowing for easy understanding and justification of the obtained results.

Acquiring knowledge, for example, from experts based on examples, is possible thanks to the inductive learning procedure. The requirements for inductive learning systems include completeness, consistency, convergence, simplicity, and the use of a minimum number of attributes. Consistently with the requirement of completeness, classification rules should describe all positive examples. System consistency means not including negative examples in the classification rules. Convergence is obtaining classification rules as a result of implementing a finite number of steps.

Different types of learning systems use various characteristic methods of knowledge representation. The initial knowledge of the system is modified as a result of the learning process. The adopted method of representing knowledge also gives rise to the principles of its modification and improvement of the system. Knowledge can be represented, for example, in the form of specific parameters of algebraic equations, logical expressions, programs, semantic networks, graphs, decision trees, or decision rules.

The currently most popular and previously mentioned neural networks are characterized by initial knowledge resulting from the selected: type of network and architecture (in other words, topology) of connections between neurons. Network architecture is most often chosen intuitively, based on previous experience with its use. Before the learning process, its unchangeable nature is assumed. The process of training the network mainly involves modifying the values of the so-called weights of individual connections between neurons. In this way, the functioning of all the neurons that make up the network changes. Knowledge is represented in most types of networks mainly by the values of these connection weights.

Neural networks have several disadvantages. One of them is the fact they require a long-term learning process. This AI method ensures relatively fast operation only at the stage of using already trained networks. One of the major disadvantages of neural networks is the so-called nonsymbolic knowledge representation obtained as a result of the training process. They belong to methods sometimes called blackbox methods. The output signals are obtained after the network processes the signals supplied to the input of this black box. Compared to the rule-based method of knowledge representation, the form of knowledge represented by the network is difficult to read for humans. This is due to the distributed and parallel processing of information by neurons included in the network and the process of creating knowledge representations as a result of modifying the connections between a significant number of neurons. The input information and its processing methods are quantitative (numerical), which significantly limits the application possibilities. In the case of neural systems, the result of the classification or forecasting process can most often be verified by comparing it with real values.

An important feature of methods enabling readable and symbolic knowledge representation methods is their qualitative form. The method of knowledge representation usually enables relatively easy implementation of an interactive dialogue with the user of this type of system, as a result of which the system generates advice, makes decisions on its own, etc. Most importantly, the advice and suggested decisions can be justified in a relatively simple way. Knowledge is stored in the knowledge base in a symbolic form, understandable to the system user.

The initial representation of symbolic knowledge can be modified as a result of the system learning process using a set of learning examples, which contains examples of concept classification – positive for a given decision-making class and negative for other classes. The information in this collection is transformed into knowledge stored in the system. Transforming information from the training set into a specific form of knowledge representation may involve, for example, the use of rote learning, analogy, deduction, and inductive learning (learning by induction). Learning from examples is called supervised learning. These examples are recorded in a decision table and described using a set of attributes relating to their characteristics expressed on numerical, ordinal, and nominal scales.

The examples analyzed during learning by induction may concern projects evaluated by experts. In the process of such evaluation, experts often use imprecise terms when referring to the assessed projects, such as good, bad, needs improvement. It is therefore difficult to formulate evaluation results in a precise way, and evaluators should clearly classify the evaluated projects. Information and knowledge about the assessed projects are granular. Depending on the possibilities, increasing the number of grains (granules) improves the precision of the evaluation. For example, instead of three grains (good, bad, to be improved), one can add the following grains: very good, very bad, that is, one can achieve an assessment accuracy of five grains. Granular computing methods are used to process information granules. Individual granules can be grouped using, for example, the criteria of coherence, similarity, and indistinguishability. Uncertain and inaccurate information can be modeled using, for example, random, interval, or fuzzy approaches.

Empirical data about evaluated projects is usually granular because the evaluation criteria have a finite number of acceptable values. In order to enable their processing in the evaluation system, a method of formal representation of this type of granular information must be chosen. The concepts of granularity, fuzzy information, and fuzzy logic are, for example, elements of fuzzy set theory introduced several decades ago (Zadeh, 1965).

In granules of knowledge-processing environments, it is possible to use not only the previously mentioned tools but also consider other solutions selected in terms of their usefulness and ease of applications. When choosing one of the methods for representing information and knowledge about projects, the ease of constructing information grains and the simplicity of knowledge representation for the implementation of a rule-based knowledge base are of key importance. Usability in practical applications of symbolic AI, as well as the related symbolic knowledge representation and symbolic learning from past experience, are of key importance.

Worth considering are the previously mentioned rough sets, in which granules of information used to describe the so-called universe (i.e., the reality related to the evaluated projects) are the smallest (basic, atomic) elements of the characteristics of a given set belonging to this universe. Therefore, it is possible to talk about granular approximation. In other words, if a given set cannot be represented as a sum of granules of information, it is a rough set (Zadeh, 2007).

From a theoretical point of view, rough sets constitute a modern mathematical tool, enabling the development of classical set theory and introducing a different approach to identifying the concept of a set created from the elements of the universe. In the case of rough sets, it is assumed that additional knowledge about the elements of the universe should be used when building such a set. Meanwhile, according to classical set theory, no such additional knowledge is needed, and a specific set is defined only by its elements that clearly belong to it. Rough sets are called the so-called undefinable sets that cannot be represented as a sum of the so-called elementary sets created from indistinguishable elements of the universe (characterized by identical information). Elementary sets and definable sets are precisely defined by the properties of the elements uniquely belonging to them. In the case of rough sets, the creator of this theory additionally introduced the concepts of lower and upper approximations of the set in order to enable their analysis. An undefinable set (rough, blurred) can be characterized by two definable sets (sharp or crisp concepts) constituting its lower and upper approximations.

From a practical point of view, a new look at the concept of a set means expanding the possibilities in the field of analysis and discovering knowledge from data. For classical set theory, it is possible to perform operations on definable concepts – for example, assign various types of projects to sets and group projects planned to be implemented within individual programs. A sharp concept is, for example, a set of projects included in a specific program, because it is possible to clearly assign projects to selected programs. In turn, the set of 'good projects' is a vague (approximate) concept because additional knowledge about individual projects is necessary to enable their evaluation and assignment to this set or another. This knowledge may also allow for the creation and analysis of an uncertain situation when a given project partially belongs to this set.

Combining Rule-Based Systems and Generative AI

The development of GAI creates opportunities to transform previously known AI systems towards increasing their functionality, productivity, streamlining analytical processes, and increasing the satisfaction of users of intelligent systems. This section responds to the need to use the capabilities of GAI integrated with RBS in AI-driven knowledge-based evaluation processes.

Research results regarding the possibilities stemming from combining the generative abilities of LLM with knowledge graphs are already known (Jovanović & Campbell, 2023). Application of such a connected AI architecture makes it possible to minimize the disadvantages and maximize the advantages of integrated solutions towards the desired quality and performance of intelligent systems. The requirements and parameters of systems using GAI can be organized into the following categories: hardware, software, and user experience (Bandi et al., 2023).

GAI systems facilitate the design and implementation of knowledge-based evaluation systems because they are user-driven technologies. These technologies are made available in such a way that they are easily accessible, which leads many people to become interested in the possibilities of AI, even though they were previously very reticent in this type of field. The integration of GAI and RBS is an opportunity to offer truly user-friendly solutions that can encourage wider use of AI in project evaluation processes. When developing detailed implementation rules, it is possible to use previous experience, for example, regarding AI-augmented digital prototyping and accelerating innovation with GAI (Bilgram & Laarmann, 2023).

The knowledge that forms the basis for project evaluation is of value to evaluators only if it is helpful and available when the need for its use arises. Thanks to GAI, knowledge can be made available in a human-friendly form, and in the case of integration with RBS systems, it additionally enhances the beneficial effects resulting from the clear form of the represented knowledge in the form of decision rules. The use of GAI can facilitate the processes of entering necessary information, which become the basis for generating rules from which knowledge bases are built. Classically, knowledge engineers are responsible for creating such knowledge bases, and thanks to GAI, their role can be reduced to a minimum.

Thanks to the integration of RBS and GAI, the processes of discovering and processing tacit knowledge can be easier. Facilitation in the implementation of these processes may result from a friendly form of information exchange between humans and the AI system using natural language. In this case, it is easier to acquire tacit knowledge in the minds of project stakeholders and expert evaluators. The implemented algorithms and IT tools are more complicated for integrated systems, but this is compensated by the usability of KBS supporting multicriteria project evaluation.

Knowledge related to project evaluation that is recorded in the knowledge base of the system combining GAI and RBS can be of the following types: about evaluation (meta-evaluation), in evaluation (concerning evaluation methods and tools), and from evaluation (resulting from evaluation processes) (Grzeszczyk, 2020). The use of an integrated evaluation system can support the ongoing updating and improvement of rule knowledge bases. This is important because tacit knowledge is relatively easily lost due to the subsequent responsibilities of stakeholders and evaluators, as well as changes in people employed in the organizations that implement subsequent projects. Phenomena related to lost knowledge and the relatively rare reuse of knowledge in subsequent projects even result in the repetition of previously made mistakes and the need to re-solve problems that have already been solved before (Coners & Matthies, 2022).

The applications of GAI are recognized and appreciated in various social and economic sectors, which justifies the need to introduce it into further solutions, also based on integration with other AI methods and systems, including RBS. Their combined use can ensure the construction and development of increasingly better KBS for the evaluation of various projects.

Building and Assessing AI-Powered Knowledge Base

The problem of building an AI knowledge base model can be formulated as follows. Available are a set of projects evaluated for possible financing and implementation, two separate subsets of projects (learning and testing), and the results of the work of experts who evaluated these projects according to an adopted set of quantitative and qualitative criteria. The answer to the following question is sought: Is it possible to implement a system model that allows project evaluation patterns to be saved in the knowledge base using the learning subset? Another question can also be asked: Is it possible to iteratively improve the evaluation process using RBS supported by GAI and LLM?

The results of the research described in this section therefore concern the AI-powered knowledge base, which stores classification patterns created using the training set. Classification patterns result from decision rules stored in the knowledge base. This base can be tested for correct evaluation using projects from the test set. The use of projects from this separate set (with known evaluation results) allows for the assessment of the usefulness of the built knowledge base and the correctness of the classification. Another issue to be explored is the possibility of iterative improvement of the evaluation process through the use of GAI and LLM.

The considerations presented in this section facilitate the creation of a formalized model that leverages the mathematical tools derived from the use of DRSA (Błaszczyński et al., 2022). In accordance with the previous assumptions, it was assumed that the knowledge base in the constructed model was to consist of decision rules. Evaluation using this database is based on the classification of projects and assigning them to one of the specific decision classes. This solution enables a clear interpretation of the results of the evaluation process. Project classification should be preceded by the system learning stage, which involves discovering knowledge – that is, generating decision rules. The process of generating rules is based on available examples – that is, historical empirical data about previously evaluated projects. The processes of generating rules and collecting knowledge are supported by GAI. Projects are assigned to specific decision classes taking into account the constantly updated database, which contains recorded knowledge about the qualitative and quantitative aspects of project evaluation.

The decision rule base (generated from examples stored in the decision table) is a finite and non-empty set of decision rules. They constitute a human-readable representation of the knowledge (obtained on the basis of project evaluation examples) necessary to carry out the process of multicriteria project sorting.

Decision rules from a knowledge base consist of an antecedent and a consequent. An antecedent is a conjunction of conditions specifying the values of specific conditional attributes. The consequent is the value of the decision attribute. To determine decision rules, a rule-generating algorithm should be used, appropriate for solving a multicriteria decision-making problem, such as the issue of project classification. This algorithm should enable solving the sorting problem of assigning evaluated projects to preferentially ordered decision classes. In the case of algorithms, various assumptions are specified a priori and experts are not required to justify their decisions a priori, based on established evaluative assumptions. The term is often used in the names of algorithms to remind us that certain assumptions have been made arbitrarily (Corrente et al., 2021). The choice of algorithm depends on the adoption of detailed implementation assumptions of the evaluation system. Based on comparative analyses, it is possible to choose from algorithms and methods based on DRSA the solution that has the most desirable properties (Greco et al., 2001; Szeląg et al., 2014).

The initial forms of decision rules can be read in the simplest way from the decision table, and a set of these rules can be created. The conditional parts of the decision rules result from the values of the evaluation criteria entered in the rows of this table. The decision parts of rules are the values of the decision attribute. Based on the empirical data recorded in the decision table, clearly defined decisions regarding specific projects that have been previously evaluated and were used to learn the evaluation system can be clearly read.

The approach used is typical for solutions to many practical problems, for which the decision table contains empirically obtained data on selected objects. Empirical data is usually imperfect, and for the evaluation problem, this may be due to the subjectivity of experts participating in previous evaluation processes, their hesitations, and their unclear preferences. Therefore, there are so-called vague concepts that cannot be clearly defined, and the analyzed projects cannot be clearly assigned to specific decision classes. The knowledge base should be constructed from a set of decision rules generated on the basis of decision class approximations. When solving a multicriteria project sorting problem, the appropriate solution is to generate a set of decision rules using previously determined upward and downward union of classes.

Decision rules can be divided into two categories: certain and possible. Certain decision rules clearly indicate decisions based on evaluation criteria that are related to the downward union of classes. In the case of possible decision rules, the decision cannot be clearly determined based on the conditional part of the rule (upward union of classes is used). Objects belonging to the lower or upper approximation are called positive examples. The set of negative examples consists of projects that are not included in a specific approximation.

In the process of generating decision rules, the so-called candidates for frequent sets are those that are supported by a number of projects equal to or greater than the minimum rule support value. Therefore, in the process of discovering strong sets, candidates whose positive support in individual union of classes is lower than the minimum value of the parameter introduced at the beginning of the knowledge base-building process are not taken into account. In addition to the concept of 'candidate for a frequent set', the concept of 'candidate for a rule' is used in the further part of the calculations.

Finding frequent sets with minimal support specified by users of computing systems is applied in various algorithms used to induce decision rules practical in solving multicriteria decision-making problems. Empirical data saved in the database can be read from it once and subjected to multiphase analysis.

First, single-element sets are analyzed. Strong sets and single-element rules are determined. In the next steps, similar calculations are performed for sets enlarged by further elements (two-element, three-element, etc.).

Decision rules are generated based on examples from the learning set, which are then used to predict the classification of projects that have not been previously used while training the system (e.g., from the testing set). The obtained decision rules and their sets can be subjected to multicriteria evaluation using the following set of indicators:

1. Length (l), size of decision rule depends on the number of elementary conditions appearing in the conjunction constituting the conditional part of the rule. For the project evaluation problem, it was assumed that the decision part always consists of one decision attribute. The length of the decision rule is usually selected experimentally and depends on the specificity of the projects being evaluated and the computational capabilities of the computer system used.
2. Absolute strength of a rule (AS) is defined as the number of objects supporting a specific rule. The parameter called 'support' is defined as the number of positive examples supporting a given rule – that is, projects from the training set for which the values of the evaluation criteria and the decision attribute are consistent with the supported decision rule. For this reason, the number of training objects supporting a given decision rule is taken into account.
3. Relative strength of a rule (RS) is determined as the ratio of AS (the number of positive examples supporting the rule) to the number of all positive examples – that is, objects belonging to the lower approximation.
4. Class of RS ($ClRS$) is an unusual parameter introduced by the author – it defines one of five ranges of values taken by the relative strength of the RS decision rule. The introduction of this parameter is justified because it facilitates the interpretation of the results obtained from the process of generating decision rules. For example, the $CLRS$ parameter can take the following five values:

$$Cl_{RS} = \begin{cases} 1\,when\ 0 \le RS \le 20 \\ 2\,when\ 20 \triangleleft RS \le 40 \\ 3\,when\ 40 \triangleleft RS \le 60 \\ 4\,when\ 60 \triangleleft RS \le 80 \\ 5\,when\ 80 \triangleleft RS \le 100 \end{cases}$$

The set of indicators presented above does not exhaust the parameters describing the generated decision rules. Other forms of these indicators can also be found in many literature items. In addition to the abovementioned rule-evaluation parameters, in the process of modeling rule systems, indicators may be useful to assess the ability of a given set of rules to predict classification. Good classification capabilities mean the usefulness of the rule-based knowledge base for implementing a multicriteria project sorting process.

The quality of a multicriteria evaluation system based on a rule-based knowledge base can be assessed using various types of indicators. A popular method of assessment is to carry out a multicriteria sorting process of test projects and determine the overall error rate, classification accuracy index, error matrix, etc.

Generally, learning the system involves generating decision rules, and the decision table is used to store empirical data regarding previously evaluated projects assigned to the training set. This collection contains classification examples representing prior project evaluation knowledge. The essence of the process of learning the evaluation system (i.e., generating decision rules) is shown in Figure 4.2.

The decision table therefore contains an initial representation of project knowledge (Table 4.1). Saving empirical data in tables is typical for various applications of rough set models and numerous generalizations of this theory. The preparation of decision tables usually precedes subsequent calculations related to the generation of decision rules, which are necessary to build knowledge bases.

The process of building an AI-powered knowledge base should be supported by GAI, which can facilitate the introduction and processing of information and knowledge in the modeled system. Thanks to the use of GAI, the system can be implemented in a way that provides greater utilitarian values and practical usefulness compared to applying only RBS. The use of innovative tools of this type creates a greater opportunity to generate solutions that are more friendly and trustworthy to potential users of such evaluation systems.

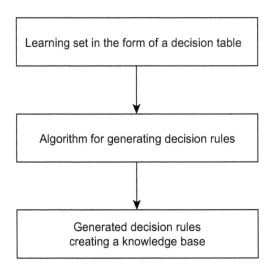

Figure 4.2 System learning sequence

Table 4.1 Knowledge system with information about projects

$U \backslash C$	Evaluation criterion c_1	Evaluation criterion c_2	Evaluation criterion c_3	...	Evaluation criterion c_m	Decision attribute d
Project x_1	$f(x_1, c_1)$	$f(x_1, c_2)$	$f(x_1, c_3)$	...	$f(x_1, c_m)$	d_1
Project x_2	$f(x_2, c_1)$	$f(x_2, c_2)$	$f(x_2, c_3)$	...	$f(x_2, c_m)$	d_2
Project x_3	$f(x_3, c_1)$	$f(x_3, c_2)$	$f(x_3, c_3)$	...	$f(x_3, c_m)$	d_3
...	...	...	...	...	...	...
Project x_n	$f(x_n, c_1)$	$f(x_n, c_2)$	$f(x_n, c_3)$	...	$f(x_n, c_m)$	d_n

Due to the above, the following principles for the operation of knowledge bases were adopted:

1. Knowledge stored in the knowledge base comes from experts who can enter data and information about their experiences related to project evaluation.
2. It is possible to consider the inclusion of NLP technology, in particular based on LLM algorithms and techniques, which can support the automation of routine tasks related to the segregation of available content and entering information into decision tables.
3. NLP techniques can facilitate the generation of real-time responses that are friendly to users of the evaluation system.
4. Updating the evaluation knowledge base for a specific type of project can be largely automated, and the role of knowledge engineers responsible for acquiring knowledge from experts and its modeling in the form of decision rules can be minimized.
5. Potential users of the modeled system should not be required to have specialized IT knowledge – that is, the ability to analyze the structures of the database and knowledge base and interfere with their content.
6. The universality of the model is ensured, which can be used to improve the evaluation of various types of projects (including those with a different number and form of evaluation criteria) and to take into account quantitative and qualitative criteria.
7. The universality of the system should also be reflected in the possibilities of improving various types of evaluation (ex-ante, ongoing, ex-post).
8. GAI chatbots can support building decision tables and knowledge bases, which should be dynamically updated based on current empirical data in subsequent iterations of improving the evaluation system.

Using Knowledge-Based Evaluation Systems

The use of a knowledge-based evaluation system should be preceded by the construction and evaluation of an AI-powered knowledge base, which was outlined in the previous section. This knowledge base can be used in classification processes concerning projects that have not previously been used during system learning.

It was assumed that a single sequence of actions repeated iteratively for the project evaluation system model consists of the following stages:

1. Determining current assumptions regarding evaluation.
2. Building a decision table (based on historical empirical data) containing objects characterizing previously evaluated projects saved in the training set.
3. Learning and generating decision rules that constitute the knowledge base about projects from the training set and constitute the basis for evaluation measures.
4. Making classification decisions using current measures (decision rules) – that is, assigning new projects to decision classes.

The implementation of the evaluation process should consist in obtaining a classification of projects by assigning individual projects to one of the precisely defined decision classes in accordance with the actual evaluation process. For example, decision classes can be adopted corresponding to the following three cases: negative substantive evaluation, positive substantive evaluation, but without current approval for financing (intended for subsequent analysis), or approval for financing and implementation.

Figure 4.3 shows the classification relationships in the decision table for three decision classes.

The problem of multicriteria sorting of objects consists in assigning individual projects to one of these decision classes. In the case of a training set, the affiliation of a given project to a specific decision class is, of course, known and presented to the system in the form of one of the learning examples.

Figure 4.4 schematically outlines the process of multicriteria project sorting – that is, assigning new projects from the test set to decision classes using a rule-based knowledge base.

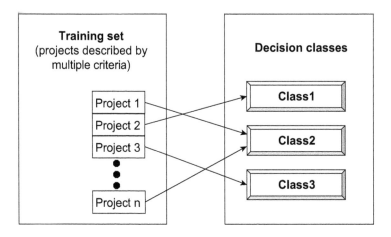

Figure 4.3 Learning examples of project classification

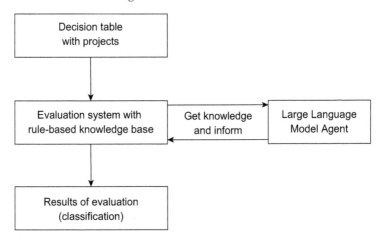

Figure 4.4 Multicriteria evaluation of projects

In knowledge-based evaluation systems, a formalized description of empirical knowledge regarding previously evaluated projects is used. According to the adopted model, the initial way of representing knowledge about projects is a knowledge system containing information about projects (also known as a decision table). Based on this table, an algorithm for generating decision rules can be implemented.

Knowledge about projects contributes to increasing skills and competences in their evaluation. Projects can be assigned to previously defined decision classes based on objects describing these projects. If knowledge is represented in the form of a table, its rows are the objects mentioned in the previous sentence, and the columns are conditional attributes. At the intersections of rows and columns one can read the values of attributes relating to specific objects.

The classification of projects means the division of the universe – that is, the set of objects describing all the studied projects. Representing knowledge in the form of a table makes it possible to replace considerations that are interesting only from a theoretical point of view with relatively simple remarks that are important from a practical point of view. Based on project data stored in tables, it is possible to develop algorithms for analyzing this data and then implement them in the form of computer applications. The use of one of the algorithms based on the DRSA enables proper understanding of the numerical values of the evaluation criteria corresponding to the numbers of points awarded during the evaluation and taking into account specific types of preferences.

Each object (project) from the decision table, belonging to the universe U, is assigned to only one decision class Cl_t belonging to the set $\textbf{\textit{Cl}}$ constituting the division U. In the considerations regarding the project sorting process, a clear division into three decision classes was adopted. This is consistent with most project evaluation processes implemented in practice. These three classes (belonging to the set **Cl**) are preferentially ordered according to their increasing importance, that is:

1. Cl_1 for projects evaluated negatively.
2. Cl_2 for projects evaluated positively but not intended for implementation because they require corrections.
3. Cl_3 for projects approved for implementation.

The decision attribute in the system learning process (generating decision rules that create a knowledge base about projects) assumes values determined on the basis of empirical historical data about previously evaluated projects. These types of objects are examples of classification for the purposes of learning the evaluation system. The set of classification examples represents previous experience in project evaluation. This set of examples stored in the rows of the decision table consists of objects (projects) described with the values of the evaluation criteria and assigned to decision classes. For each decision class Cl_t a set of training examples E_{Clt} is therefore stored in the decision table DT. This set consists of objects (projects) $x \in U$. Two types of parameters are assigned to each of them, that is:

1. Evaluation criteria (the assumption was made that all attributes are criteria $a_i \in A$), values of an information function in the following form $(f(a_1, x), f(a_2, x), \ldots, f(a_m, x))$.
2. Decision attribute $f(d, x) = Cl_t$.

In the process of supervised learning of the system, an information table can be used extended with the decision attribute d to form a decision table. The decision attribute specifies information about how to divide the objects (projects) into specific decision classes.

As mentioned above, decision classes belonging to the **Cl** set are ordered preferentially, according to the increase in their importance. The superiority of one of the objects (projects) over the other means better values for the conditional and decision criteria. Determining approximations in a way typical of the CRSA is therefore pointless. This is explained with an illustrative example later in this section.

In the case of DRSA, the following unions of classes are used (Greco et al., 1998):

1. Upward union of classes – at least Cl_t is marked as $Cl_t^{\geq}$.
2. Downward union of classes – at most Cl_t is marked as $Cl_t^{\leq}$.

Theoretically, there can be n union of classes. In order to simplify the considerations regarding the project evaluation process and to make the results more useful in practical applications, in this description the value of n is taken as three.

A graphical interpretation of the union of three classes is shown in Figure 4.5.

Downward unions of classes $Cl_t^{\leq}$		
$Cl_1^{\leq}$		
	$Cl_2^{\leq}$	
		$Cl_3^{\leq}$
Projects from class 1	Projects from class 2	Projects from class 3

Upward unions of classes $Cl_t^{\geq}$		
		$Cl_3^{\geq}$
	$Cl_2^{\geq}$	
$Cl_1^{\geq}$		
Projects from class 1	Projects from class 2	Projects from class 3

Figure 4.5 Unions of classes

Assuming the value of *n* equal to three, it is possible to formulate certain union of classes properties that are useful in the process of modeling the evaluation system, that is:

1. $Cl_1^{\geq} = Cl_3^{\leq} = U$ – these are unions of classes that take into account all possible decisions, so there is no point in determining this union for the purposes of calculating parameters for the evaluation process.
2. $Cl_2^{\geq} = U - Cl_1^{\leq}$ and $Cl_3^{\geq} = U - Cl_2^{\leq}$ (e.g., all projects that cannot be included in the class Cl_3 or better are classified as Cl_2 or worse).

As previously mentioned, according to the DRSA instead of attributes, as in the case of CRSA, there are criteria with a domain of attribute values ordered according to specific preferences. This enables data analysis that is useful in evaluation systems because projects are evaluated based on these types of criteria. Attributes appearing in the CRSA can also take on numerical values (seemingly resembling the number of points awarded for individual evaluation criteria). However, they do not take into account the preferential order necessary to consider the dominance of some projects over others.

Further within the text illustrative examples of decision tables containing empirical data will be presented, constituting a practical justification for the use of the selected DRSA instead of, for example, the CRSA. The three conditional attributes (understood as criteria) have domains consisting of four values: $B = \{6, 7, 8, 9\}$. Projects described by these criteria are clearly assigned to three decision classes corresponding to situations occurring in the actual process of evaluating this type of project. Therefore, in this example, a variant characteristic for this type of problem was adopted, with one decision attribute taking on three values intuitively associated with the project evaluation process. This attribute determines the classification of projects defined by the set of decision classes $\boldsymbol{Cl} = \{Cl1, Cl2, Cl3\}$. The decision attribute corresponding to Cl_1 means a low assessment of the application for project financing (from the point of view of its specific features). This value of the decision attribute means that a decision has been made to reject the application by the expert evaluating the given project. The other two values taken by this attribute should be understood similarly.

In order to obtain good readability of the presented illustrative examples, integer values of the evaluation criteria were adopted, which are evaluated on a scale from zero to ten points, and the preference increases with the increase in the number of points. The presentation of these examples uses project data collected during the author's previous research (Grzeszczyk, 2012).

The data was chosen to clearly present the usefulness of the selected DRSA. It is worth noting that, unlike many algorithms for generating decision rules based on the CRSA in the case of DRSA-compliant algorithms, it is not necessary to carry out a preliminary data preparation procedure (continuous – quantitative attributes), known as the so-called discretization. This is important from the point of view of practical applications of the DRSA trend. Quantitative values of project evaluation criteria, which constitute the number of points awarded by experts evaluating projects, are relatively often used.

In the case of many algorithms consistent with the CRSA without a discretization procedure, for quantitative attributes, it is not possible to find relationships between data using the indiscernibility relation. Therefore, in most cases, this approach requires a discretization procedure to determine a specific number of value intervals of equal width based on the domain of numerical (continuous) attributes. These designated intervals can be assigned symbolic codes using discretization methods (Grzymala-Busse & Stefanowski, 2001). However, the use of such methods involves some computational effort and may be a source of errors. Thus, the option not to use this procedure is advantageous and reflects well on the chosen DRSA.

The preferential order in the field of values of criteria describing projects means that the Cl_3 should be dominant over the Cl_2. The decision criterion with the value Cl_3 is the most preferred decision class. In turn, the Cl_2 should be dominant over the Cl_1. Cl_1 is therefore the least preferred decision class. Higher values of the class designation number are consistent with increased preferences.

Table 4.2 shows the lower and upper approximations of the Cl_3 determined in accordance with the CRSA (projects *p3 . . . p6*). The lower

Table 4.2 Lower approximation and boundary region according to CRSA

	Projects creating the universe U	Evaluation Criterion c_1	Evaluation Criterion c_2	Evaluation Criterion c_3	Decision Attribute d
	p_1	6	8	6	Cl_1
	p_2	6	6	6	Cl_1
Lower approximation	p_3	9	8	9	Cl_3
	p_4	9	9	9	Cl_3
Boundary region	p_5	7	7	8	Cl_3
	p_6	7	7	8	Cl_2
	p_7	7	6	8	Cl_2
	p_8	6	6	7	Cl_2
	p_9	7	6	7	Cl_1

approximation of the decision class of the adopted projects is shaded, and the boundary region of this class is marked using a bold frame. Reasoning intuitively, it is possible (for projects $p3$ and $p4$) to construct a decision rule determined by the lower approximation of class, that is, the rule in the following form:

IF $k3 = 9$, then the decision attribute certainly belongs to Cl_3 (the project is accepted for implementation).

This type of certain decision rule clearly determines the value of the decision attribute based on the value of the criteria.

The decision rule supported by the upper approximation of class does not make it possible to determine a clear decision based on the criteria. It only constitutes the so-called possible decision rule in the following form:

IF $k_2 = 7 \wedge k_3 = 8$, THEN decision attribute probably belongs to Cl_3 and the project can probably be accepted for implementation.

The above possible rule was built using projects $p5$ and $p6$ from the boundary region. They constitute (together with the $p3$ and $p4$ projects) an upper approximation of the Cl_3. In turn, using only the boundary region leads to the construction of a differently interpreted possible decision rule (sometimes referred to as an approximate decision rule), that is:

IF $k_2 = 7 \wedge k_3 = 8$, THEN the decision attribute belongs to Cl_2 or Cl_3. In such a case, the project is evaluated positively substantively or accepted for implementation.

Due to the fact that possible decision rules are a source of doubt and have relatively little practical significance, they were omitted in further considerations regarding the construction of the evaluation system model. It was limited to certain decision rules based on the lower approximation.

Table 4.3 Comparison of CRSA and DRSA for the multicriteria project sorting problem

	Projects	c_1	c_2	c_3	d	Direction of preference changes
	p_3	9	8	9	Cl_3	
	p_4	9	9	9	Cl_3	
Border region for CRSA and DRSA	p_5	7	7	8	Cl_3	Not compliant with the dominance principle
	p_6	7	7	8	Cl_2	
	p_7	7	6	8	Cl_2	
Border region for DRSA (not for CRSA)	p_8	6	6	7	Cl_2	Not compliant with the dominance principle
	p_9	7	6	7	Cl_1	
	p_1	6	8	6	Cl_1	
	p_2	6	6	6	Cl_1	

The illustrative example shown in Table 4.3 shows the need to use the selected DRSA. In this approach, it is possible to take into account the principle of dominance. This table sorts the previously analyzed data (from Table 4.2) in descending order from the point of view of the order of preferential decision-making attributes (from the best decision class to the worst). The boundary region for CRSA and the DRSA are highlighted (in bold border). The directions of preference changes inconsistent with the principle of dominance were also marked.

The semantic correlation between the criteria and the values of the decision attribute means that (according to the principle of dominance) improving one of the criteria (e.g., increasing the number of points awarded by the expert from 6 to 7) should not result in a deterioration of the final project evaluation (with the other criteria values unchanged). When comparing the pairs of projects (projects $p5$, $p6$ and $p8$, $p9$) from Table 4.2, one can notice the occurrence of inconsistencies with the principle of dominance. This is explained below.

Using the CRSA it is possible to build (based on the $p8$ and $p9$ projects) the following two certain decision rules:

1. IF $k_1 = 6 \wedge k_3 = 7$, THEN the decision attribute certainly belongs to Cl_2 and the project is positively evaluated substantively.
2. IF $k_1 = 7 \wedge k_3 = 7$, THEN the decision attribute certainly belongs to Cl_1 and the project is completely rejected, that is, negatively evaluated substantively.

The lack of practical usefulness of the above decisio n rules obtained using the CRSA consists in the deterioration of the value of the decision attribute (contrary to the principle of dominance) when one of the criteria is improved. Projects p_8 and p_9 are characterized by the same values of criteria k_2 and k_3. In the case of a project belonging to the least preferred decision class Cl_1, the k_1 criterion is higher. This happens quite often in practice. This situation should be properly taken into account in the evaluation process using a knowledge base composed of decision rules. These rules should therefore be generated using an algorithm based on the DRSA.

In the case of projects p_5 and p_6, two different values of the decision attribute are obtained for equal values of conditional criteria, which also goes against the principle of domination.

When conducting a multicriteria analysis of two projects, the dominance of the criteria values should also cause dominance due to the decision attribute values. It is intuitively understandable that a project evaluated better by experts (as a result of assigning higher values to its criteria) should be assessed better also from the point of view of assigning it to a higher decision class. It is obvious that a project with lower criteria values cannot be accepted for implementation instead of a project with higher criteria values.

For example, in the case of projects p_5 and p_7 there are no contradictions with the principle of dominance. Project p_5 dominates over p_7 because: $f(k_2, p_5) = 7 > f(k_2, p_7) = 6$ (with the same values of the remaining criteria), and project p_5 was included in the more preferred decision class, that is, $f(d, p_5) = Cl_3 > f(d, p_7) = Cl_2$.

Using the above experiments, it is possible, for example, to determine the dominant and dominated sets for the p_6 project, necessary to determine the union of classes approximations in accordance with the DRSA. These collections are similar in nature to the so-called elementary concepts known from the classical theory of rough sets.

A set of projects (described by a set of conditional criteria B) dominated by p_6: $D_B^-(p_6) = \{p_1, p_2, p_6, p_7, p_8, p_9\}$.

In turn, the set of dominant objects p_6: $D_B^+(p_6) = \{p_3, p_4, p_5, p_6\}$.

The assignment to decision classes results from the three values taken by the decision attribute d. Therefore, the unions of classes are as follows:

1. Downward union of classes $Cl_1^\le = \{p_1, p_2, p_9\}$, $Cl_2^\le = \{p_1, p_2, p_6, p_7, p_8, p_9\}$.
2. Upward union of classes $Cl_2^\ge = \{p_3, p_4, p_5, p_6, p_7, p_8\}$, $Cl_3^\ge = \{p_3, p_4, p_5\}$.

The union of classes described above is graphically presented in Tables 4.4 and 4.5. The markings in these tables are as follows: The darker shading is the lower approximation of the union of classes (downward or upward), and the lighter shading is the B-boundary region of the downward or upward union of classes.

Table 4.4 Approximations for downward union of classes

Projects	c_1	c_2	c_3	d
p_3	9	8	9	Cl_3
p_4	9	9	9	Cl_3
p_5	7	7	8	Cl_3
p_6	7	7	8	Cl_2
p_7	7	6	8	Cl_2
p_8	6	6	7	Cl_2
p_9	7	6	7	Cl_1
p_1	6	8	6	Cl_1
p_2	6	6	6	Cl_1

Border region: $\{p_8, p_9\}$. $Cl_1^{\leq}$

Projects	c_1	c_2	c_3	d
p_3	9	8	9	Cl_3
p_4	9	9	9	Cl_3
p_5	7	7	8	Cl_3
p_6	7	7	8	Cl_2
p_7	7	6	8	Cl_2
p_8	6	6	7	Cl_2
p_1	6	8	6	Cl_1
p_2	6	6	6	Cl_1
p_9	7	6	7	Cl_1

Lower approximation. $Cl_2^{\leq}$

Table 4.5 Approximations for upward union of classes

Projects	c_1	c_2	c_3	d
p_3	9	8	9	Cl_3
p_4	9	9	9	Cl_3
p_5	7	7	8	Cl_3
p_6	7	7	8	Cl_2
p_7	7	6	8	Cl_2
p_8	6	6	7	Cl_2
p_9	7	6	7	Cl_1
p_1	6	8	6	Cl_1
p_2	6	6	6	Cl_1

Border region: $\{p_8, p_9\}$. Lower approximation. $Cl_2^{\geq}$

Projects	c_1	c_2	c_3	d
p_3	9	8	9	Cl_3
p_4	9	9	9	Cl_3
p_5	7	7	8	Cl_3
p_6	7	7	8	Cl_2
p_7	7	6	8	Cl_2
p_8	6	6	7	Cl_2
p_1	6	8	6	Cl_1
p_2	6	6	6	Cl_1
p_9	7	6	7	Cl_1

$Cl_3^{\geq}$

The abovementioned tables also mark the lower approximations (and border regions) of these unions of classes as follows.

1. For downward union of classes

   - $\underline{B}(Cl_1^{\leq}) = \{p_1, p_2\}$, $\overline{B}(Cl_1^{\leq}) = \{p_1, p_2, p_8, p_9\}$, $Bn_B(Cl_1^{\leq}) = \{p_8, p_9\}$,
   - $\underline{B}(Cl_2^{\leq}) = \{p_1, p_2, p_7, p_8, p_9\}$, $\overline{B}(Cl_2^{\leq}) = \{p_1, p_2, p_5, p_6, p_7, p_8, p_9\}$, $Bn_B(Cl_2^{\leq}) = \{p_5, p_6\}$,

2. For upward union of classes

   - $\underline{B}(Cl_2^{\geq}) = \{p_3, p_4, p_5, p_6, p_7\}$, $\overline{B}(Cl_2^{\geq}) = \{p_3, p_4, p_5, p_6, p_7, p_8, p_9\}$, $Bn_B(Cl_2^{\geq}) = \{p_8, p_9\}$,
   - $\underline{B}(Cl_3^{\geq}) = \{p_3, p_4\}$, $\overline{B}(Cl_3^{\geq}) = \{p_3, p_4, p_5, p_6\}$, $Bn_B(Cl_3^{\geq}) = \{p_5, p_6\}$.

By determining approximations of the unions of classes in the above way, it is possible to determine sets of projects $BN_B(Cl_t^\leq)$, $BN_B(Cl_t^\leq)$ that belong to the boundary region and inconsistent with the principle of dominance.

It is worth noting that specific projects are not permanently assigned to boundary regions. For example, projects p_8 i p_9 (Table 4.4) cannot be taken into account when determining certain rules in the case of $Cl_1^\leq$ because they then belong to the boundary region. However, they can be taken into account for $Cl_2^\leq$ because they then belong to the lower approximation.

The union of classes approximations determined in this example are then used in the process of generating decision rules. As previously mentioned, certain rules are induced based on the objects in the lower approximation. Possible rules generated using the upper approximation and possible rules determined from the boundary region are omitted.

Taking into account the research conducted on knowledge-based evaluation systems, the following can be concluded:

1. It is advisable to search for new systems ensuring improvement of project evaluation, which can complement the previously used simple models of multicriteria evaluation performed by experts.
2. The proposed evaluation model enables increasing objectivity and simplifies the project evaluation process.
3. It is possible to develop an evaluation model based on the integrated approach, GAI and RBS, the knowledge base of which can be improved as a result of knowledge discovery through learning using a set of projects saved in the learning set.
4. The proposed model can constitute the basis for developing its practical implementation in the form of computer-assisted improvement of an AI-driven knowledge-based evaluation system.

It is desirable to continue research related to combining RBS, GAI, and AI-driven knowledge-based evaluation. Potential areas of application of this type of evaluation systems are management of commercial, public, and development projects. The proposed solutions can be used both in the processes of planning and management of development projects, as well as their evaluation at many levels of selection and multicriteria classification made by organizations deciding on their financing.

References

Amin, H., Scheepers, H., & Malik, M. (2023). Project monitoring and evaluation to engage stakeholders of international development projects for community impact. *International Journal of Managing Projects in Business*, *16*(2), 405–427. https://doi.org/10.1108/IJMPB-02-2022-0043

Bandi, A., Adapa, P. V. S. R., & Kuchi, Y. E. V. P. K. (2023). The power of generative AI: A review of requirements, models, input – output formats, evaluation metrics, and challenges. *Future Internet, 15*(8), 260. https://doi.org/10.3390/fi15080260

Bilgram, V., & Laarmann, F. (2023). Accelerating innovation with generative AI: AI-augmented digital prototyping and innovation methods. *IEEE Engineering Management Review, 51*(2), 18–25. https://doi.org/10.1109/EMR.2023.3272799

Błaszczyński, J., Greco, S., Matarazzo, B., & Szeląg, M. (2022). Dominance-based rough set approach: Basic ideas and main trends. In S. Greco, V. Mousseau, J. Stefanowski, & C. Zopounidis (Eds.), *Intelligent decision support systems* (pp. 353–382). Springer International Publishing. https://doi.org/10.1007/978-3-030-96318-7_18

Budhiraja, S., Yadav, M., & Rathi, N. (2023). Multi-level outcomes of learning organisation: A bibliometric analysis and future research agenda. *Journal of Organizational Effectiveness: People and Performance*. https://doi.org/10.1108/JOEPP-02-2023-0039

Chai, J., Weng, Z., & Liu, W. (2021). Behavioral decision making in normative and descriptive views: A critical review of literature. *Journal of Risk and Financial Management, 14*(10), 490. https://doi.org/10.3390/jrfm14100490

Coners, A., & Matthies, B. (2022). Perspectives on reusing codified project knowledge: A structured literature review. *International Journal of Information Systems and Project Management, 6*(2), 25–43. https://doi.org/10.12821/ijispm060202

Corrente, S., Greco, S., Matarazzo, B., & Slowinski, R. (2021). Explainable interactive evolutionary multiobjective optimization. *SSRN Electronic Journal*. https://doi.org/10.2139/ssrn.3792994

Deal, N. M., Hartt, C. M., & Mills, A. J. (2023). *ANTi-history: Theorization, application, critique and dispersion*. Emerald Publishing Limited. https://doi.org/10.1108/9781804552414

Divasón, J., Martínez-de-Pisón, F. J., Romero, A., & Sáenz-de-Cabezón, E. (2023). Artificial intelligence models for assessing the evaluation process of complex student projects. *IEEE Transactions on Learning Technologies, 16*(5), 694–707. https://doi.org/10.1109/TLT.2023.3246589

Fernandes, D., & Machado, C. F. (2021). The misconception between organizational learning and knowledge management. In C. Machado & J. P. Davim (Eds.), *Knowledge management and learning organizations* (pp. 137–170). Springer International Publishing. https://doi.org/10.1007/978-3-030-71079-8_7

Fridgeirsson, T. V., Ingason, H. T., Jonasson, H. I., & Jonsdottir, H. (2021). An authoritative study on the near future effect of artificial intelligence on project management knowledge areas. *Sustainability, 13*(4), 2345. https://doi.org/10.3390/su13042345

Gamel, J., Bauer, A., Decker, T., & Menrad, K. (2022). Financing wind energy projects: An extended theory of planned behavior approach to explain private households' wind energy investment intentions in Germany. *Renewable Energy, 182*, 592–601. https://doi.org/10.1016/j.renene.2021.09.108

Greco, S., Matarazzo, B., & Slowinski, R. (1998). A new rough set approach to evaluation of bankruptcy risk. In C. Zopounidis (Ed.), *Operational tools in the management of financial risks* (pp. 121–136). Springer US. https://doi.org/10.1007/978-1-4615-5495-0_8

Greco, S., Matarazzo, B., Slowinski, R., & Stefanowski, J. (2001). An algorithm for induction of decision rules consistent with the dominance principle. In W. Ziarko & Y. Yao (Eds.), *Rough sets and current trends in computing* (Vol. 2005, pp. 304–313). Springer Berlin Heidelberg. https://doi.org/10.1007/3-540-45554-X_37

Griffin, R. (2021). *Fundamentals of management* (10th ed.). Cengage Learning.

Grzeszczyk, T. A. (2012). *Modelling evaluation of European projects*. Placet (In Polish).

Grzeszczyk, T. A. (2020). Capturing tacit knowledge in evaluation of development projects. *Proceedings of 21st European conference on knowledge management*. 21st European Conference on Knowledge Management. https://doi.org/10.34190/EKM.20.097

Grzymala-Busse, J. W., & Stefanowski, J. (2001). Three discretization methods for rule induction. *International Journal of Intelligent Systems, 16*(1), 29–38. https://doi.org/10.1002/1098-111X(200101)16:1<29::AID-INT4>3.0.CO;2-0

Haass, O., & Guzman, G. (2020). Understanding project evaluation – a review and reconceptualization. *International Journal of Managing Projects in Business, 13*(3), 573–599. https://doi.org/10.1108/IJMPB-10-2018-0217

He, Q., Tian, Z., & Wang, T. (2022). Performance measurement methods in megaprojects: An analytical review. *International Journal of Project Management, 40*(6), 634–645. https://doi.org/10.1016/j.ijproman.2022.05.009

Joullié, J.-E., & Gould, A. M. (2023). Theory, explanation, and understanding in management research. *BRQ Business Research Quarterly, 26*(4), 347–360. https://doi.org/10.1177/23409444211012414

Jovanović, M., & Campbell, M. (2023). Connecting AI: Merging large language models and knowledge graph. *Computer, 56*(11), 103–108. https://doi.org/10.1109/MC.2023.3305206

Kerzner, H. (2022). *Project management: A systems approach to planning, scheduling, and controlling* (13th ed.). Wiley.

Klapper, H., Maciejovsky, B., & Puranam, P. (2021). Influence structures and information aggregation in groups. *SSRN Electronic Journal*. https://doi.org/10.2139/ssrn.3858423

Lee, R. W. (2022). Knowledge management and the learning organization. In J. Chen & I. Nonaka (Eds.), *The Routledge companion to knowledge management* (1st ed., pp. 67–79). Routledge. https://doi.org/10.4324/9781003112150-6

Luxmi. (2014). Organizational learning act as a mediator between the relationship of knowledge management and organizational performance. *Management and Labour Studies, 39*(1), 31–41. https://doi.org/10.1177/0258042X14535158

Midler, C., & Alochet, M. (2023). Understanding the Phoenix phenomenon: Can a project be both a failure and a success? *Project Management Journal*, 875692782311718. https://doi.org/10.1177/87569728231171825

Montrosse-Moorhead, B. (2023). Evaluation criteria for artificial intelligence. *New Directions for Evaluation, 2023*(178–179), 123–134. https://doi.org/10.1002/ev.20566

Patton, M. Q. (2018). Evaluation science. *American Journal of Evaluation, 39*(2), 183–200. https://doi.org/10.1177/1098214018763121

Patton, M. Q., & Campbell-Patton, C. E. (2021). *Utilization-focused evaluation* (5th ed.). SAGE Publications, Inc.

Rode, A. L. G., Svejvig, P., & Martinsuo, M. (2022). Developing a multidimensional conception of project evaluation to improve projects. *Project Management Journal, 53*(4), 416–432. https://doi. org/10.1177/87569728221095473

Rutherford, H. (2022). Perspectives on complex system governance performance. In C. B. Keating, P. F. Katina, C. W. Chesterman, & J. C. Pyne (Eds.), *Complex system governance* (Vol. 40, pp. 339–363). Springer International Publishing. https://doi.org/10.1007/978-3-030-93852-9_12

Sales, X. (2019). A proposed methodology for evaluating the quality of performance management systems. *Pacific Accounting Review, 31*(3), 376–393. https://doi.org/10.1108/PAR-03-2018-0019

Samset, K., & Volden, G. H. (2022). Closing the loop. In T. M. Williams, K. Samset, & G. H. Volden (Eds.), *The front-end of large public projects* (1st ed., pp. 158–190). Routledge. https://doi.org/10.4324/9781003257172-7

Santhose, S. S., & Lawrence, L. N. (2023). Understanding the implementations and limitations in knowledge management and knowledge sharing using a systematic literature review. *Current Psychology, 42*(36), 32427–32442. https://doi.org/10.1007/s12144-022-04115-6

Scriven, M. (1991). *Evaluation thesaurus* (1st ed.). SAGE Publications, Inc.

Serrador, P., & Turner, R. (2015). The relationship between project success and project efficiency. *Project Management Journal, 46*(1), 30–39. https://doi.org/10.1002/pmj.21468

Szeląg, M., Greco, S., & Słowiński, R. (2014). Variable consistency dominance-based rough set approach to preference learning in multicriteria ranking. *Information Sciences, 277*, 525–552. https://doi.org/10.1016/j.ins.2014.02.138

Szwarcfiter, C., Herer, Y. T., & Shtub, A. (2023). Balancing project schedule, cost, and value under uncertainty: A reinforcement learning approach. *Algorithms, 16*(8), 395. https://doi.org/10.3390/a16080395

Uddin, S., Ong, S., & Lu, H. (2022). Machine learning in project analytics: A data-driven framework and case study. *Scientific Reports, 12*(1), 15252. https://doi.org/10.1038/s41598-022-19728-x

Zadeh, L. A. (1965). Fuzzy sets. *Information and Control, 8*(3), 338–353. https://doi.org/10.1016/S0019-9958(65)90241-X

Zadeh, L. A. (2007). Granular computing and rough set theory. In M. Kryszkiewicz, J. F. Peters, H. Rybinski, & A. Skowron (Eds.), *Rough sets and intelligent systems paradigms* (Vol. 4585, pp. 1–4). Springer Berlin Heidelberg. https://doi.org/10.1007/978-3-540-73451-2_1

5 Conclusions

Correctly conducting multifaceted evaluations has a decisive impact on the proper planning and implementation of various types of projects, as well as the effective achievement of organizational goals. The knowledge-based evaluation system model indicates one of the possible directions for developing comprehensive approaches and methods, which may contribute to improving the quality and objectivity of planning, evaluation, and project management processes. It is worth noting that AI technologies, particularly intelligent generative systems, are playing an increasingly important role in modern business. This book synthesizes key issues and challenges related to developing AI applications in project management. The proposed knowledge-based evaluation is implemented with the support of an integrated approach, knowledge discovery through learning, GAI, and several concepts affecting contemporary management. Inspiration from various approaches and ideas makes it possible to consider quantitative and qualitative aspects in the comprehensive evaluation of projects. The proposed solution fundamentally differs from classic evaluation approaches in business project management, which are mainly based on simple financial measures.

Project management is a dynamically developing and recognized field within business and management. This book highlights the opportunities arising from conducting transdisciplinary research and drawing on the rich achievements in developing research on KBS that can be used to support project evaluation processes comprehensively. The use of the proposed solutions creates good conditions for the implementation of multifaceted and knowledge-based evaluation processes.

The synthetically presented research results confirm that using an integrated methodological approach enables the multifaceted classification of various projects, considering their difficult-to-measure and qualitative elements. The developed evaluation model also allows for taking into account unstructured factors relating to the specific features of individual projects and the evaluators' knowledge resources – that is, their education, experience, and attitudes. The results obtained from the research also constitute a reliable basis for determining the following theoretical and practical effects.

DOI: 10.4324/9781003341611-5

The theoretical achievements consist of obtaining the following results:

1. Selected AI technologies used in business and project management were reviewed.
2. The possibility of developing evaluation systems resulting from the use of machine learning, rough set models, KBS, and GAI was indicated.
3. An attempt was made to comprehensively approach the problem of improving project evaluation using an integrated methodological approach, which makes it possible to consider both quantitative and qualitative criteria, which cannot be analyzed solely in strictly financial and economic aspects.
4. Attention was drawn to the advantages of using the DRSA approach in the process of constructing a rule model of a knowledge discovery system useful for continuous improvement of multicriteria project sorting.
5. The possibilities of combining RBS and GAI in solving the multicriteria problem of project evaluation based on learning systems were indicated.
6. The need and possibility of discovering the tacit knowledge of experts as a result of computer-aided inference and classification of information and knowledge have been demonstrated.
7. The possibility of including empirical knowledge from experts who evaluated previous evaluation processes recorded in the knowledge base in the current project evaluation was proposed.
8. A knowledge-based evaluation system was suggested to provide computer support for decision-making based on empirical knowledge and to objectify, simplify, and accelerate the project evaluation process.
9. It was proposed to use learning methods and adaptive evaluation metrics as decision rules in the iterative model.

The practical research results described in this book include the following achievements:

1. The need to build and implement a model of the system based on evaluation knowledge was demonstrated, in which decision rules are generated using a learning set consisting of projects previously evaluated by experts.
2. The basis was created for the implementation and empirical verification of the model of the evaluation system with a knowledge base used to evaluate projects that had not previously been used to build knowledge base.
3. The practical usefulness of the decision table was indicated to collect information and knowledge and obtain an initial representation of knowledge about previously evaluated projects.
4. It was proposed to represent evaluation knowledge in a practically helpful, readable symbolic form (decision rules), and assumptions were developed to build tools for generating these rules.
5. A model of a system based on empirical knowledge was developed, constituting a generalization of experts' experiences related to the classification

of projects, enabling the management of such knowledge and use in the project evaluation process.

6. It has been shown that the system model allows for considering quantitative and qualitative criteria that are difficult to measure.

7. It was pointed out that the proposed model of a knowledge-based learning system enables the management of empirical expert knowledge, adaptive, flexible, and intelligent improvement of the project evaluation process.

8. Identifying projects inconsistent with the principle of dominance was proposed to facilitate the detection of probably erroneous decisions of experts evaluating projects.

9. It has been shown that there is a need to perform evaluation using a computer representation of expert knowledge with justification for the decisions made regarding the assignment of projects to specific decision classes in the form of generated decision rules.

The presented concept of a knowledge-based evaluation system can be used to design various types of systems introduced to improve project evaluation. They may support the implementation of tasks faced by the management staff of public and commercial organizations, which should undertake activities related to the comprehensive improvement of project evaluation to ensure the organization's sustainable development in the conditions of globalization and turbulent environment.

The basis for using research results to improve multicriteria project evaluation systems in various organizations was created. Solutions characterized by practical usefulness were proposed. Using a rule-based evaluation improvement system based on expert knowledge may contribute to obtaining economic benefits calculated at an individual level, in diverse organizations, and even in entire knowledge-based economies.

The research results justify the need for further development of interdisciplinary research in this field, and other research may address the following issues:

1. Expanding the model with the ability to analyze the suitability of individual evaluation criteria in order to reduce unnecessary calculations.

2. Supplementing the developed model by taking into account (in the process of improving the initial evaluation) data from ex post evaluation regarding the results obtained after the completion of the projects.

3. Improving the mechanisms for assessing the quality of the model and knowledge base by increasing the number of parameters for assessing the generated decision rules.

4. Analyzing the networking issue of the developed model and examining the possibilities of developing the implementation of a project evaluation system made available on the Internet for training and methodological purposes.

5. Considerations of modifications of the mathematical apparatus used and comparative analyses of the effectiveness of algorithms for generating decision rules and solutions based on LLM.
6. Development of research related to the huge potential of GAI and LLM.

Particularly interesting are the prospects for developing research on evaluation systems in the context of growing opportunities related to GAI and LLM. Ideas regarding the combined use of these innovative AI and RBS technologies are also interesting. Building and updating rule-based knowledge bases are not easy tasks. Knowledge-based evaluation systems should be universal and enable the evaluation of various types of projects. Different sets of projects are usually characterized by multiple evaluation criteria. Modifications in evaluated projects should often be associated with significant changes in the content of knowledge bases. Failure to adequately update these knowledge bases undoubtedly leads to misclassification of projects.

The use of LLM and GAI allows for efficient and quick updating of knowledge bases with the necessary data in an automated manner and with little involvement of knowledge engineers, whose labor costs are usually high and such specialists are typically difficult to access. It needs to be remembered that knowledge saved in knowledge bases should concern the principles, criteria, and evaluation of projects, which are not subsequently evaluated. Knowledge-based evaluation systems ought to generalize the acquired knowledge and enable the classification of projects that were not previously the basis for learning these systems.

The concept of RBS and GAI integration creates the basis for developing research on more reliable intelligent evaluation systems that can be regularly and continuously updated regarding the correctness of knowledge bases. Using LLM agents can be helpful in quickly improving knowledge bases and reducing project classification errors.

In addition to the undoubted advantages, it is worth mentioning the disadvantages of LLM agents, which are characterized by the uncertain nature of knowledge sources, and it is often difficult to prevent the so-called hallucinations. In the case of GAI and LLM, there is no clear distinction between valuable domain knowledge from specific sources and uncertain knowledge from unknown sources. Using LLM agents dedicated to particular tasks is usually expensive and often requires undertaking time-consuming preparatory tasks to perform the appropriate ones. The costs of maintaining and operating such advanced models will continue to increase. It is, therefore, worth considering the economic calculation and profitability of implementing such advanced solutions. In particular, the need to implement an integrated RBS and GAI solution with LLM should be carefully considered. Before making such significant investments, it is worth considering maintaining and updating them in the long term.

Implementing evaluation systems based on an integrated approach is an idea to be realized in the long term. As far as functionality is concerned, RBS used for project evaluation works quite well. However, it is worth considering the selection of an appropriate knowledge discovery algorithm, which should be selected in terms of reducing the information resources required, accelerating calculations carried out in the process of improving project evaluation, taking into account the impact of the length of generated rules, the minimum size of the training set sufficient for an effective learning process, and the elimination of redundant rules etc.

Carrying out further research on knowledge-based evaluation systems may create conditions for modeling the improvement of project evaluation in a broader scope. This approach to the currently presented issues enables further research on modeling improvement of evaluation towards truly holistic and comprehensive solutions.

There is a growing interest among practitioners in scientific solutions to the problem of multifaceted evaluation of contemporary projects, which often require considering phenomena and quality criteria that are difficult to quantify. A significant contribution to scientific research in this area has been achieved thanks to the proposed solutions based on extensive achievements in the field of AI, data science methods, and GAI. The content presented in this book may also be valuable outside the scientific community due to the practical usefulness of the considerations devoted to taking into account in project evaluation aspects that are difficult to measure and presented qualitatively in the form of decision rules. Research on the implementation of GAI in this area is at an early stage of development, and this book can be a synthetic introduction to the implementation of further research related to AI-driven knowledge-based evaluation.

Index

Note: Tables are indicated in **bold,** and figures in *italics.*

Milton Keynes UK
Ingram Content Group UK Ltd.
UKHW031137141024
449569UK00006B/113